Time's Best Jewel

The Too-Short Life of Richard Michael Barad, M.D.

Wayne T. Dilts

To Danielle—
First, my student. Now
my friend. How lucky can a
guy get? I hope you enjoy this.
Wayne T. Dilts

DEDICATION

For Leah Barad who never had the chance to know her father.

Contents

Prologue

"On the death of a friend, we should consider that the fates through confidence have devolved on us the task of a double living, that we have henceforth to fulfill the promises of our friend's life also, in our own, to the world."

~ Henry David Thoreau
Journal, February 28, 1840

Dick Barad

Forward

"So, why do you want to write this book?"

Richard "Dick" Barad and I were classmates in high school during the 1960s in northwestern New Jersey. He was an adventurous, intensely intelligent, handsome, driven, opinionated, and fun-loving young man who took pleasure in living every day. He attracted people to him by his smile, intense eyes, and easy disposition. He knew what was right and what was wrong - if you didn't believe as he did, you were wrong - and he accepted challenges with enthusiasm. He became a world traveler, an activist, and a man passionate about causes close to his heart. He was goal-oriented. He knew that in order to succeed he had to study, a chore for which he had unwavering patience. He decided he would become a doctor like his father and big brother. He succeeded in virtually everything he set out to do. He graduated Cornell University, like his father had done; became a primary care physician; married the second serious girlfriend he ever had; spent a year with his wife as missionary doctors in Africa; set up a family medical practice in Vermont; and become a father to a beautiful baby girl.

And through it all, I never knew of anyone who did not like him.

Dick worked very hard for his successes. He seemed to set his goals early in life without much anguish, and was willing to do whatever it took to achieve them. He had incredible discipline: he could study all day, or night, if need be. Some of his friends were potheads but he did not indulge. He knew his own mind and beliefs, and he was not influenced negatively by anyone for any reason.

In fact, Dick lost only one battle in his life, and it was against a disease that would not be defeated. At 33 years old, and just two weeks before his daughter's first birthday, Richard Michael Barad, M.D., lost his brief yet bitter battle with brain cancer.

He was brave in the face of his fate, but that was a tendency shared with his siblings. Younger brother Bob would later classify the Barad children as "fearless" in a way that led each of them to explore life to its fullest. Dick embraced each new goal in his life as a challenge to be met without fear. In fact, the only time Dick expressed any fear was not of dying, but of "being forgotten." He did not want to be remembered for his death but for how he lived his life.

His baby daughter never had the chance to know him, to remember his face or his voice or his touch. She grew up yearning for more information than she had, but most of the people who knew her father best were scattered around the country and, indeed, around the world. She has very little to remember him by.

Thus, this book.

Dr. Gerald "Jerry" Barad, M.D. and Beatrice "Bea" Krival Barad were Dick's father and mother, an interesting and compelling couple. Both were raised in Brooklyn, New York, just a few miles apart. Where Bea was more of a "free spirit," Jerry was much more stoic. Bea stood just over five feet tall, Jerry was 6' 4". Bea became a college graduate with a degree in cytology (that branch of biology that deals with cell formation, structure, and function) and a lab technician at a time when few females had a post-secondary education. Jerry became a doctor specializing in OB/GYN in the 1950s when it was still an evolving science. He was also a biologist and took an intense interest in all living plants. Bea devoted herself to her family when they had children; Jerry became one of the leading gynecologists in the greater metropolitan New York area. They were an "odd couple" in that they seemed to be so different, but their deep abiding love for each other and their family made that union work.

As with many married couples, they came to be known as one entity – "JerryandBea" – "DrandMrsBarad" – "momanddad".

They had four children: David Hyman Barad, the oldest son, was born in 1950; Richard Michael "Dick" Barad was born in 1952; Dorothy Bonnie "Dot" Barad, the only girl, in 1954; and Robert Alan "Bob" Barad, the youngest, in 1959.

For our first discussion about this book project, Jerry and Bea invited me to join them at their home in Hunterdon County, New Jersey, one weekend afternoon in early June, 2011. While they were preparing dinner in the kitchen, Dot gave me a tour of the grounds of their homestead. I had been there only once before, and that had been 41 years earlier, so most of it seemed new to me.

The sliding glass doors lead to the back yard and open onto a very wide concrete and brick porch. The view of the property from that porch is breathtaking. The yard slopes away from the house in a southerly direction, down a hill that runs about a quarter of a mile to a pond far below. It is an impressive sight with a gorgeous view.

The wide concrete steps were the starting point for the remarkable winter sled rides you will read about shortly. The steps lead down into the back yard, and the first things I noticed were the many different garden spots throughout the yard with a plethora of flowers in full bloom. We walked past the swimming pool and made our way to Jerry's "pride and joy" – two very extensive greenhouses that were filled literally to the roof with hundreds (and hundreds) of varieties of cactus and succulent plants.

We made our way back towards the pool and sat by the koi pond for a short while. Jerry poked his head out of the house and yelled to Dot that it was okay with him if she wanted to feed the many (and large) koi. She did. Every few seconds a lawn sprinkler would automatically come on. The sprinkler, Dot explained, helped chase away any predator birds that had their eyes on the koi.

I was astounded at how much time and detail Jerry had put into the creation of this back yard. Below the pool (in the middle of the sled run, Dot explained) he had put in a large garden, and some of the plants were beginning to sprout.

We were summoned inside.

Jerry and Bea first served a roast beef dinner before we talked about the book project. We were joined by older brother David, and I felt strange, as if I were taking Dick's place at the dinner table 50 years earlier. After dinner and small talk among the Barads, Bea turned to me and said point blank with a bit of a rough edge in her voice: "So, why do you want to write this book?" … as if to say, "Why do we need to go back over all those memories again?" My answer apparently satisfied her:

In October, 2010, I was on the organizing committee for the 40th reunion of the Hunterdon Central High School (HCHS) Class of 1970 of which Dick Barad and I were members. The other three members of the committee were classmates Barbara Funk, Debbie Hooper, and Jody Arvanitides. (Each of the three ladies has been married, but I use their maiden names here.) At our reunion, more than 100 of our 420 classmates attended. The committee decided to hold a memorial tribute to the 30 members of our class who had already passed away, including Dick, by lighting a candle and announcing each name.

Dick's brother David was a member of the HCHS Class of 1968; Dot was two years younger than Dick, and a member of the Class of 1972. Most of our classmates knew both David and Dot, and since Dick had been the president of our student council during our senior year (1969-70), we felt it was appropriate to invite them to the reunion and ask them to say a few words during the memorial. They agreed.

David read a very moving speech he had written about how much he still missed his little brother 25 years later, and there were many wet eyes in the room when he was done. (See the complete speech in Appendix I). Then Dot took the microphone and, speaking more impromptu than David, said one thing that resonated with me more than anything else that night. Dot said, "Just before Dick died, he expressed to me that he was afraid that he would be forgotten after he was gone."

As I related this comment, Jerry said, "I remember him saying that." You could have heard the proverbial pin drop.

I turned to Mrs. Barad at that moment and said something along the lines of, "That comment chilled me. I went home and thought about it for a couple of months. It wouldn't go away. As a teacher of English for 24 years, I know that if it is committed to paper, it cannot be forgotten. Dick was my friend. I can't let that happen to him. And his daughter never knew him. She has the right to know her father as we knew him."

I stopped talking. So did everyone else.

I really don't remember exactly what happened next, but I know that I told them why I thought I was qualified to do this project: I had been a newspaper reporter for two years and won some writing awards from the New Jersey Press Association, I had taught writing at the high school level for 24 years, I had edited my father-in-law's autobiography in 2007 (*Just The Way It Was* by Thomas Gilrane), and I had written a two-act stage adaptation of

4

Hawthorne's *The Scarlet Letter* (2000). I didn't try to sound boastful, but I conveyed to them that I had the credentials to take on and complete this project. And, besides, Dick had been a friend of mine.

But one additional advantage, I felt, was that I had not been a close friend of Dick's. We met in high school. He was in the pit band. I was on stage. He was tremendously popular. I was voted "Class Apple Polisher." We ran in different circles. But, I considered him a friend.

Shortly after we graduated from high school in June, 1970, a new singer/songwriter named Jim Croce became very popular, seemingly overnight. Number one hits such as *Time in a Bottle* and "Bad, Bad Leroy Brown" skyrocketed Croce to international fame. He was always new, producing folk songs of hope and love and loss that resonated with an ever-cynical society in the days of Viet Nam and Richard Nixon. We came to feel as if Croce was singing to each of us, individually, revealing secret feelings in our young lives and making us, along the way, huge fans.

It seemed that Croce and his music had been around forever, and we were looking forward to that kind of relationship for decades to come. But our Crocean world shattered on September 20, 1973, with the horrible news of his death in a plane crash in Louisiana. We were devastated, stunned, numb. Croce left behind a widow and a two-year-old son.

For Croce, the rise to superstar was meteoric. But he had been working as a singer and songwriter for years. He was driving a truck when his wife Ingrid told him she was pregnant. That night he sat down and wrote *Time in a Bottle* and decided to give this music career one more serious try.

The parallels between Jim Croce's life and the life of Dick Barad may seem like a stretch to some, but consider this: While Dick didn't become world famous or fabulously wealthy, he did touch many lives – as a son, as a brother, as a doctor, as a family man, as a friend. He established his own medical practice – his breakthrough – but it only lasted two years, as did Croce's superstardom. Dick left behind a dazed and confused widow, as well as a beautiful baby that he did not get the chance to enjoy as she grew up. And both died in September. Again, not compelling comparisons, but enough for me to draw a picture for Dick's daughter, Leah, that the father she never knew was a rock star of life, that he was as committed to becoming the best doctor he could possibly be, just as truck driver Croce committed himself to becoming a musician on the day he found out his wife was pregnant.

Jim Croce and Dick Barad's shining stars burned very brightly, however briefly, and their impact is still being felt, 40+ years later.

As I left the Barad household that early June afternoon, I knew that if I did not have their confidence, this project would come to a grinding halt.

A few days later I got an email from Dot: "They liked you. You're in."

So here we are.

Chapter 1

Jerry and Bea
"Life is for the living."

Once I had the Barad's permission, the floodgates of family history opened to me.

When Jerry Barad and Bea Krival were children, they did not know each other, even though they only lived about two miles apart in Brooklyn, New York: the Barad family lived in Manhattan Beach, while the Krival family lived in Bensonhurst. Dick Barad's great grandfather David Barad emigrated from Russia in 1892 with a promise of a job that turned out not to exist. His wife Adele would follow soon after. Bea's parents emigrated from the Ukraine, then also a part of Russia, in 1921. Jerry and Bea met at a summer camp that was part of the Hashomer Hatzair Zionist movement when they were 14 years old, in 1937.

Jerry was an imposing and handsome figure: tall with a bushy head of hair and a commanding baritone voice that had the power of decades of leadership behind it. He ran a tight ship, and always did, according to his children. He had an inquisitive nature: he took medical courses at times when he didn't have to simply to satisfy his curiosity. He co-founded the New York Cactus and Succulent Society in the 1950s and took his wife and children on adventures in deserts and swamps around the country looking for samples to bring home. He always had a greenhouse of sorts. His first was a small one in the recess of a dormer window in Brooklyn. The last were the two large structures that he had built in the 1960s in the back yard in Hunterdon County that still stand today. According to daughter Dot, Jerry has the largest private collection of cacti and succulent plants in one single indoor location in the world.

Each year for 60 years, Jerry and Bea hosted an annual open house to members of the Cactus and Succulent Society that drew busloads of collectors and the curious to their home. Admirers viewed and sometimes purchased samples of the hundreds of varieties that Jerry had grown over the decades.

Bea was "Jeff" to Jerry's "Mutt," but she was the "tallest" person in her family. She had a strong voice and a keen mind. In her presence, one never felt that she was a short person – her personality added more than inches to her stature. She was a college graduate with a BA in Biology, the science near and dear to her husband's heart as well. She was a collector of an eclectic assortment of things: for some unknown reason, Bea kept a picture of the ancient Egyptian Queen Nefertiti over her bed that had appeared on a cover from Time magazine. And was a staunch believer in her mantra, "Life is for the living."

As a boy, Jerry attended children's classes at the Brooklyn Botanical Garden where he learned how to plant vegetables. In 1940, Jerry applied to Cornell University in Ithaca, New York, and he was accepted into the College of Agriculture. It was not easy for a "city kid" to be accepted into the Agricultural School, but Jerry attributed his acceptance in large part to the recommendation written by his teacher at the Brooklyn Botanical Garden, Mrs. Ellen Eddy Shaw. Another advantage to the Agricultural School was that there was no charge for tuition as opposed to the $600 tuition that was charged in the School of Arts and Sciences.

After two years, however, and at his father's urging, Jerry switched majors and became a pre-med student. It was also a time when the country was involved in World War II, and Jerry enlisted in the Reserve Corps. He was called up at the end of his junior year, in 1943.

Jerry served his basic training at Camp Grant in Illinois in an Army medical unit. After basic, he was assigned to the pathology lab at Walter Reed Army Hospital outside of Washington, D.C., where he spent about a year "cleaning mortuary tables and assisting in autopsies," in his own words. However, it was there that he learned how to cut tissue for microscope slides. He also developed an interest in parasites, and so he signed up for a night course in parasitology at George Washington University at his own expense.

He was then assigned to Fort Lewis near Seattle, Washington, where he spent nearly a year before being assigned to the 29th Medical Laboratory Unit that was going to be the command laboratory in India for the China-Burma-India Theatre. He shipped out of California and spent between 5-6 weeks zig-zagging across the Pacific to avoid German and Japanese submarines.

When his ship sailed into the Ganges River delta in India, Jerry felt as if they had sailed back in history by about a thousand years. The river was lined with palm trees and they were met by ships with brightly-colored sails and four oarsmen at the helm. This was colonial India prior to its independence from Britain.

Jerry's company was headquartered in New Delhi and was called a "casual company" in that they were counted at reveille and then again at night. The reason it was so "casual" was due to the atomic bombs that had recently been dropped on Japan that had ended the war.

Jerry was working in one of the labs in India. He recalled one day his assignment was to take a 6-hour train ride north to a small town of Kasauli where he had to pick up eight cages of white lab rats and return with them to camp. He still recalls the looks he received when he hired locals to carry the cages, complete with rats, on their heads back to the camp. Jerry also got to play Santa Claus that year, riding into camp on a camel.

When Jerry returned to the states in early 1946 after 33 months of service in the Army, he knew that he wanted to marry Bea, so he proposed by mail before his return. Bea had graduated from Hunter College in the spring of 1945 and was working at New York Presbyterian Hospital as a lab technician. Jerry and Bea got married on June 23, 1946, when they were both 23 years old.

They returned to Ithaca that fall so Jerry could complete his undergraduate degree, which he earned the following spring. Bea worked at a hospital in Ithaca while Jerry studied. They lived in one room in a rooming house off campus, and one of the other residents was a man named Tishman, who would go on to become the future Manhattan real estate tycoon.

Jerry knew he wanted to go on to medical school and he applied to continue his studies at Cornell University medical college. He was turned down. There had been more than double the usual number of applications to medical school that year due to the number of returning veterans.

Undeterred, Jerry scheduled a meeting with Dean Edwards of the medical school. "I told him how much I wanted to continue my studies in med school at Cornell University," Jerry explained, "and asked him point blank how I could improve so that I could get accepted on the next application." The Dean told Jerry that he needed better grades in language and math.

Jerry & Bea-September 2013

Chapter 2

Manhattan, NYC (1947 – 1954)
"David and Dickie"

In the fall of 1947, Jerry and Bea moved to Manhattan and Jerry enrolled in New York University graduate school to improve his skills in the areas of language arts and math, as Dean Edwards had recommended. They lived in an apartment of 6 or 7 small rooms for $75 month in a building at 118th Street and Morningside Drive, where Columbia University would later build the International Affairs building (420 W 118th Street). Bea took a job as a lab technician at Cornell Medical Center Lying-In Hospital (Note: when New York Hospital-Cornell Medical Center opened in 1932, the Lying-In Hospital became the Obstetrics and Gynecology Department of New York Hospital, occupying one of the pavilions along the East River in the upper 60s in Manhattan. Ed.)

One day Bea saw a line of men waiting for their interviews to get into Cornell Medical Center's med school. Bea walked in and asked if Jerry could get an interview. The clerks in charge checked their paperwork and came back to her and said, "He doesn't have to. He's already been accepted." Jerry didn't receive the paperwork in the mail for several days, but they celebrated nonetheless.

Jerry's first internship was at Lenox Hill Hospital in the upper 70s and Park Avenue in Manhattan. There he rotated in different departments every couple of months. He stated his interest in Obstetrics. William Stutteford was his attending physician and his style of training was, according to Jerry, "to train fewer extremely well" rather than the norm, which was "to train many not so well." Jerry flourished and became senior intern during his first year.

Bea and Jerry's first son, David Hyman Barad, was born a week after Jerry's 27th birthday, on March 29, 1950, at Cornell Medical Center Lying-In Hospital.

When Jerry was finishing up his internship, Dr. Stutteford recommended that Jerry do his residency at Bellevue Hospital at First Avenue and 27th Street in Manhattan.

Of the ten interns that applied, Jerry was appointed Resident at Bellevue. It was a three-year position, and during his first year, he was placed in charge of the OB/GYN pathology laboratory. He also rotated with the OB senior resident and the GYN senior resident on calls. One of the other doctors on rotation at Bellevue was Dr. Herman Rannells, who also had a practice in a new rural hospital out in Hunterdon County, New Jersey. Rannells worked at Bellevue one day a week.

Richard Michael Barad was born April 21, 1952, also at Cornell Medical Center Lying-In Hospital when Jerry was starting his OB/GYN residency. David was two years old when Dickie (as he was called in his earlier years) was born.

The apartment house across the street from the Barad apartment on 118th Street was where David and Dickie had friends, Peter and Liza Mahr. Their mother, Stella, was from Iceland and became friends with Bea. Jerry was in his last years of medical school, internship year and first year of residency while they lived here.

Jerry raised tropical fish in a big fish tank in his study. Sometimes he drove to the Jersey swamps to collect daphne plants to feed the fish. He sometimes used to sell the daphne to tropical fish stores.

Dick was an infant and a toddler at that apartment. David went to nursery school at Riverside Church at 490 Riverside Drive and his mother walked him there across the Columbia University campus. The boys played in Morningside Park, which covered 13 blocks along Morningside Drive, from 110th Street to 123rd Street. At some point during this time, they became "DavidandDickie," one entity.

In 1956, Bea and Jerry spent a week in Mexico and the boys were left with a baby sitter for the entire week. This was scary for the young boys. When their parents returned, they brought many souvenirs with them. David and Dickie each received a puppet, Peanut and Jocko. There were no ownership issues over which puppet belonged to which boy: just as they were known as "David and Dickie," the puppets were "Peanut and Jocko," and they belonged to both. They learned how to work the puppets and put on puppet shows for years.

Chapter 3

Manhattan Beach, Brooklyn (1954-1957)
Scratchy and Genie

Dot was born on February 11, 1954, also at Cornell Medical Center's Lying-In Hospital. Shortly thereafter the family moved out of Manhattan and into grandfather Alex's house at 218 Beaumont Street in the Manhattan Beach section of Brooklyn. David remembers Dorothy ("we never called her 'Dot' when we were young") as a baby when they brought her home from the hospital, specifically that her fingers were so small. They lived on the second floor. Dick and David shared a room in the back of the house and Dorothy's room was next to theirs.

Dick and David became friends and playmates with other kids on the street, and David's best friend was Andy. At the end of the block was a concrete esplanade that was partially broken up by earlier hurricanes. They could walk along the waterfront to Manhattan Beach or to Brighton Beach and then Coney Island. David recalls that the boys took that walk more than once. One specific memory when David was six years old and Dick was four has them standing in front of the Parachute Jump on Coney Island, but they were too short to ride. They had walked down by themselves and later had to walk back, a distance of about two miles. David is not sure if they ever told their mother about that trip.

The waterfront under the esplanade held large mica schist boulders that the water crashed upon. David and Andy and Dick often went to the area to play. David and Andy were six years old and felt it was safe for them but they were afraid that Dick was too small to climb on the rocks safely. To scare Dick away from the rocks, they told him that there were ferocious water rats in the rocks and that the rats had eaten another (fictional) Barad brother. In remembering this years later, David felt that they were mean to scare him but that it did keep him off the rocks. Dot remembered that the adults used to tell them to "beware of the undertow" which the kids misinterpreted to mean "beware of the under toad." They were scared that a huge toad might come out and get them.

In the summer, they went to the end of the block to watch fireworks every Tuesday from Coney Island. They burned punks to keep the mosquitoes away.

Sometimes groceries were delivered from their grandmother's grocery store, and the boys thought it was great because the groceries came in boxes. Dick and David once fashioned the boxes into a "kitchen" for Dorothy, making a cardboard stove and refrigerator.

The boys attended Hebrew School at the Manhattan Beach Jewish Center at 60 West End Avenue, a short walk from their home. It was on a walk back from Sunday School one day that they found a litter of kittens behind a hedge on the side of the road. They picked out a calico kitten that they took home and named Scratchy. Later Scratchy had kittens herself and one of them was an orange tomcat that they kept and named Genie. The boys' grandmother was a bird lover and she hated the cats because the cats would scratch her carpet.

Dick and David slept in bunk beds, with David taking the top. The cats slept with them: Scratchy with David and Genie with Dick. When they were going to sleep, Dick and David made up stories for each other, with Tony the Tiger of Kellogg's Frosted Flakes fame ("They're grrrrrreeeeaaaattttt!") often the hero of these stories.

Their father had an old Stella guitar that he did not know how to play but he strummed it and often sang "Good night children." He also made up stories to tell them when they went to sleep. "I'll tell you a story of Jack and his glory and now my story's begun." If he were asked right away to tell them another story, he would say, "I'll tell you another of Jack and his brother and now my story is done."

This memory was an odd one, David recalled, because their father was rarely home during his residency.

While they were living there, Jerry built a small "greenhouse" in the front dormer window of the living room and another small greenhouse in the back off his bedroom.

The whole family used to eat dinner watching television in the parents' bedroom, enjoying such popular shows as The Mickey Mouse Club with "Spin and Marty," Circus Boy, and Superman. David claims they virtually never missed an episode of Superman, remembering the tag line, "Truth, Justice, and the American Way!" Bea used to make lamb chops grilled in the broiler or chicken drumsticks that they called "polkas."

Grandfather Alex was only home some of the time due to marital difficulties, but when he was home he would build projects with the grandchildren. He had a Chia head that they tried to grow hair on. After Grandpa Alex grilled steaks in the back yard, he always cut up the steak into small pieces so the children would not choke on them. Grandmother Mildred grew a patch of mint near the back door. She always had seltzer in the old-fashioned bottles and had syrup that could sweeten it. She even had an electric dishwasher, and David never understood why she rinsed the dishes before putting them in the dishwasher. What was the point of the dishwasher if she washed the dishes first?

Shari Lewis, the puppeteer, gave a show at the Jewish Center when Dick was either three or four years old. David remembers that he, his mother, and Dick went to the show. At one point Ms. Lewis asked for volunteers from the audience and although everyone raised a hand, she picked out Dick. Shari Lewis had Dick help with a few tricks and gave him some balloon animals. David recalled being jealous.

Dick had reddish brown hair and a small pug nose when he was young. His mother thought he looked Irish and she called him "Richard McRichard." Dick went to nursery school while they lived in Manhattan Beach, when he was two or three years old. One day his teacher called Bea to say that she thought Dick had a slight speech impediment. Bea responded rather indignantly that he had just started speaking a month or so before.

Bea had a friend, Roberta Baskin, who lived a block away from Shore Boulevard and had a son Louis, who was Dick's age, and a younger daughter Beth, who Dot remembered as her first friend. Their father Milt was a pharmacist. For Dot's third birthday, the Baskins gave her a Tiny Tears doll. It became her favorite doll and Dot still owns it.

A few blocks from the Baskin home was a walking bridge that crossed Sheepshead Bay that some people used to fish from. There were also fishing boats on the other side of the bay that people could buy fresh fish from when they docked in the evening. Dick and David sometimes fished off the sidewalk, but never off the bridge because the bridge was too high. David remembers one time catching a porgy, a very bony fish. When he took it home, Bea broiled it for him but it was too difficult to eat.

There was a famous fish restaurant just across this bridge called Lundy's where the children's parents would go out to dinner. Sometimes Bea brought home the lobster claw to show the kids what the claw looked like.

As with any seaside, there was a strong breeze off the ocean. For a while, Jerry went through a kite-making phase. He made kites out of bamboo and paper and the family flew them together. Once he made a huge kite six feet tall that he had to fly with heavy line. Even though he was a big man, in a strong breeze that big kite could pull him around. David remembered one day the big kite flew dangerously close to an apartment building on the west side of Oriental Boulevard. The kite stayed in his grandmother's garage for many years after that incident.

Meanwhile, Jerry was completing his residency at Bellevue Hospital in lower Manhattan while the family lived in Brooklyn. Sometimes Bea would drive the children up to Bellevue to visit him. The drive took them down the Belt Parkway past all the numbered warehouses. Dick and David used to count down the numbers. After one such visit, while they were returning home, a car going in the opposite direction lost control and went over the divider, landing on the hood of the Barad's car. They were all taken to Lutheran Hospital in Brooklyn. Bea needed stitches on her left knee from hitting the emergency brake handle and Dorothy had a butterfly bandage on one eyebrow. Dick and David were shaken up but were not injured.

While the family lived in Manhattan Beach, the New York City Aquarium opened and David recalls going there with the family.

One winter, Jerry bought a sled and sometimes pulled the children along on the street. There were small hills in front of the houses sliding down to the street, but only about five feet long. The children longed for a real sledding hill. Little did they know that in a few short years they would have a sleigh-riding hill that became the envy of all their friends. But they would have to move to New Jersey first.

Chapter 4

Disneyland
"Are we there yet?"

Children's television changed forever on October 27, 1954, at 7:30 p.m. EST, when ABC television broadcast the very first episode of a new show for children called *Disneyland*. Walt Disney was trying to find ways to finance the construction of his dream theme park in California. He thought that he could broadcast a television show that would appeal to children to raise the $17 million he needed to build Disneyland. He took the idea to the then-struggling ABC television network, and they agreed to broadcast a one-hour show. *Disneyland*, as the show was called, became a fixed landmark on the viewing schedule of more than 12 million households by the following June.

Characters like Davy Crockett entered the Barad family lives. Dick and David waited anxiously all week for the next episode of Davy Crockett to be broadcast. They even had coonskin caps and watches and memorized the Davy Crockett song.

Jerry finished his time at Bellevue in 1957 and, to celebrate, he planned to take the family on a cross country drive to California. As far as David, Dick, and Dot were concerned, the only purpose of the trip was to visit the Disneyland theme park. They were barely through the Lincoln Tunnel when Dot (three years old) began asking if they were at Disneyland yet.

The family of five drove Alex's 1952 Buick Special through the tunnels of the Pennsylvania Turnpike as they headed to Chicago. They sometimes camped and other times stayed in hotels. In Chicago, they visited Jerry's cousin Gilbert and stayed overnight at his home. Gilbert had built a geodesic dome-like jungle gym for his kids and Dick and David enjoyed climbing on it.

Then they made their way to Salt Lake City, Utah. They swam in the Great Salt Lake and were impressed at how easily they floated on the water. Crossing the Rocky Mountains, they stayed in a small cabin one night, and in the morning Jerry took the children to a trout fishing pond where they caught trout that he prepared for a late breakfast.

During the entire trip across country, the children sang their favorite songs. David sang *The Davey Crockett* theme song, Dick sang *The Ballad of the Boll Weevil* and Dot's song was *My Pigeon House*. David remembers that Dick had some difficulty with altitude sickness as they crossed the Continental Divide.

When they made a stop in the desert so that Jerry could look for cactus plants, all three children joined in the hunt. Dick suddenly yelled, "I found a bone!" He had found a pair of antlers that were proudly displayed in their house for decades.

As they crossed the mountains for a descent into California via the Donner Pass, the car started making an odd ca-chunk noise coming from the back. They pulled over but Jerry could not diagnose the problem, so they kept going down the winding mountain road. This was one of those roads with a sheer rock wall on one side of the road and a drop-off cliff on the other. Ca-chunk chunk chunk and the car started moving faster. It turned out the sound was coming from the rear axle and eventually the axle broke and the car was moving downhill coasting without brakes.

Jerry and Bea remembered it as kind of scary, but the children were in the back seat waiting to get to Disneyland and were not aware of any danger. Eventually Jerry saw a copse of trees on the side of the road that did not end in an immediate drop-off. He ran the car into the trees (which turned out to be Arbor Vitae – the Tree of Life) and they did not fall down the cliff. However, all the luggage on the roof rack did.

No one was injured and they got out of the car and surveyed the damage. While they were sitting on the grassy side of the road waiting for help, Dot was stung by a bee, the only injury of the day.

The first stop in California was not Disneyland but rather a Cactus and Succulent Society convention in San Francisco. To the children, it seemed like it lasted a week. They met some interesting people, including Slim Morton (who was responsible for some of the western landscaping at Disneyland). David remembered that they went to a lot of luncheons and drank iced tea with lots of sugar in it. They also visited cactus nurseries before eventually making it to Anaheim and Disneyland.

While at Disneyland, the children met Roy from *The Mickey Mouse Show* and he drew charcoal pictures for each of them: he drew Mickey Mouse for David, Dick got a drawing of Donald Duck, and Dot got one of Minnie Mouse. They rode on the African Adventure and went on a Trip to Mars on the TWA rocket in Tomorrowland. Dot remembers riding on the Dumbo ride, and that David thought it was too babyish for him and Dick, so Jerry went on the ride with her, which made it even more special.

The children do not remember the ride back to New York, but Dot does remember being happy to be home. The happiness, however, was short-lived. Soon after their return they began packing for the move 60 miles west of Brooklyn, out to Flemington, New Jersey, the county seat of Hunterdon County.

Both David and Dot remember being upset about leaving Beaumont Street because they were moving away from their friends. But their father had accepted a part-time job in a new regional hospital center in rural New Jersey.

Chapter 5

The Hunterdon Medical Center
"$114 for the cause"

In 1946, Hunterdon County was predominantly rural and agricultural, and was the only one of the 21 counties in New Jersey that did not have a hospital to service its approximately 40,000 residents. Attempts had been made during the previous 30 years to create a local hospital in Hunterdon but for a variety of reasons each effort failed.

In late 1945 and early 1946, a local committee was formed that did extensive research into "the enormous expansion of health services throughout the nation, which had, to a great extent, bypassed rural areas. Attention was called to disparities in rural health and mortality, as well as in infant and maternal death rates" (Katcher 28).

On July 3, 1946, this local committee submitted their findings in a report to the Hunterdon County Agricultural Board. The report pointed out that hospitals in surrounding counties were being stretched to their capacities by being forced to serve the approximately 4,000 Hunterdon residents that required hospital services each year. The report recommended that Hunterdon either help "enlarge and improve neighboring hospitals or 'build… a hospital of our own' "(29).

That report set in motion a series of events that ultimately became the Hunterdon Medical Center (HMC), which opened its doors exactly seven years later to the day: July 3, 1953.

Part of the federal post-World War II Hill-Burton legislation helped to finance the construction of hospitals in areas where none existed. That legislation paid for one-third of the cost if the community raised the other two-thirds (HCD. 25 June 1953, sec V, 1).

To apply for Hill-Burton funds, the hospital had to be incorporated, which it was on March 25, 1948, with a broad spectrum of Hunterdon residents represented on the Board of Directors.

One of the primary supporters and a member of the Board was local farmer Lloyd Wescott, who served on many committees in many capacities throughout New Jersey. Wescott was instrumental in acquiring funding for the new hospital. "In February 1947, the N. J. Departments of Institutions and Agencies .... gave Hunterdon top priority for federal aid for construction (of the new medical center)." The chairman of that state committee was Wescott (Katcher 55).

In early 1947, Edward Lewinsky Corwin, Ph.D., was hired to create a report on the type of hospital HMC should become and the costs involved. He was considered an expert in the field since he had, "(I)n 1946, ... completed a (national) survey of American hospitals" (59). During 1947, he compiled a report on what HMC should be, reflecting the results of his survey. What he proposed, and what was accepted, was that HMC would be more than just a "medical hotel:" it would be a regional hospital with resident experts in a variety of fields and that it would have an association with a medical college and a city hospital as well (HCD. 25 June 1953. Sec V, 1).

The projected cost, however, seemed prohibitive: $1.8 million (about $20 million today). To take advantage of the federal Hill-Burton funding, the county would have to raise $1.2 million, or $114 per family then living in the county, a seemingly impossible task (HCD. Ibid).

What followed was an outpouring of support from across the county, a grassroots movement to raise the money needed to build the hospital. Granges and churches held fund-raising dinners. Shoeshine boys set up a site in front of the Union Hotel on Flemington's Main Street to raise $114 for the hospital. At one point, more than 10,000 of the 12,000 families in the county had contributed financially. Of the first $1.5 million raised, 20% of the donations were in increments of less than $100 (Katcher 77-80).

Back in 1954, when Jerry was beginning his training at Bellevue Hospital in Manhattan, he met Dr. Herman Rannels who "worked one day a week in gynecological pathology" (321), an interest Jerry shared. Rannels was then the chief of Obstetrics at the newly-opened Hunterdon Medical Center out in New Jersey, and Rannels shared stories of working at HMC that intrigued Jerry. After Jerry finished his residency in 1957, he accepted an offer from Rannels: when Jerry came back from the Disneyland trip with his family, he would go to Hunterdon and cover for Rannels for six weeks while Rannels went on vacation. When Rannels returned, he offered Jerry a part time position as the second doctor in OB-GYN at HMC. Jerry accepted (321).

David & Dick

Chapter 6

Darts Mills
Getting "countrified"

When the Barad family returned from their trip to California and Disneyland, David remembers driving out to Flemington a few times from Brooklyn when his parents started looking for a place to live there. The trip seemed long, though not too long compared to the recent drive back and forth to California.

In preparation for the move the family held a small sidewalk sale in Brooklyn. "I remember not selling much except the peacock feathers that we had brought back from California," David recalled. "I also remember that Dad was upset that we sold the peacock feathers."

David also vaguely remembers all of them crowding into his father's old Blue Buick Special and leaving Manhattan Beach for the last time.

According to David, "Dad never sold or traded-in his old cars. He continued to use the old '52 Buick Special with foam seats and electric windows until we moved to Sandbrook. The car was parked in one of the sheds that used to stand above where the greenhouse stands, just east of the pool. The car continued to be stored there for another 20 years until the shed was demolished to make room for a shade garden. While it stood there with its grill pointing out of the shed two small saplings grew in front of it. One sapling was just next to the front fender and as it grew the fender pushed into it. When they took down the shed the fender was buried halfway into a 10-inch trunk, so they had to cut the fender to move the car."

Jerry and Bea did not find a place for the five of them to live right away. Instead, they spent the end of the summer at a small motel at Darts Mills, a designated area off Route 523, also known as the Whitehouse-Flemington road to those who lived in the area. Darts Mills is located at a bend in the South Branch of the Raritan River about three miles north of Flemington. The bend in the river backs into an area that was a natural swimming hole. There were several small cabins that made up the motel, and a makeshift beach with a slide and a swing into the river water. There were speakers playing the popular music during the day, including songs such as "The Purple People Eater" and "Itsy Bitsy Teeny Weenie Yellow Polka Dot Bikini." (*According to Google, "Purple People Eater" topped the charts in 1958, which established the year they moved out there*). David was 8, Dick was 6 and Dot was 4. They had brought their cats, Scratchy and Genie with them. Bea was just 35 and David remembers some of the older kids telling him that they thought she was pretty. "Mom dressed a little Bohemian so she probably did make an impression," David recalled.

Dot remembers: "We lived at Darts Mills for the first summer we were in New Jersey. I only have vague memories of it... mostly remember my Dad fishing with my brothers and my pole and line was a stick with a string and a pin that didn't even reach the water...so I never caught anything. That and the 'motel' had a row of doors that all looked the same to me so when I stepped outside the door I was never sure which one my family was behind. That's scary when you're four years old."

Jerry went to work at the new hospital about a mile away, but when he came home each afternoon, he and the kids went fishing in the Raritan River. They brought a pail of big worms called "nightcrawlers" that Jerry had collected back in Brooklyn. To collect worms, Jerry attached two long nails to an electric cord and put the nails in the ground about a foot apart. He then plugged the cord in and the worms crawled out of the ground. They had hundreds of worms in a pail of moist earth and they brought the worms with them from Brooklyn. The sunfish loved the worms and by the end of the first week they had a big pail of sunfish. The boys from the other cabins started accompanying them and at the end of the week they had a big fish fry with all the neighbors. David recalls that this kind of event went on almost weekly for the rest of the summer.

The railroad tracks cross the Raritan River about a half mile from Darts Mills. Dick and David became friendly with the other boys and one afternoon they "hiked" to the railroad bridge. The boys would stand underneath the bridge while the train rolled overhead.

The family attended their first Flemington Fair while they were living in Darts Mills. The Flemington 4-H Agricultural Fair was held at the Flemington Speedway outside of town for seven days at the end of the summer, ending on Labor Day. It had begun in 1865 by the Hunterdon County Agricultural Society. By the late 1950s, it included many breeds of animal judging, farm machinery exhibits, 4-H exhibits of most types of vegetables and animals, and a "Midway" with many loud carnival rides and attractions and food vendors.

The Barad children especially loved all the farm machinery that they could climb all over and sit in the drivers' seats. When they had lived in Brooklyn, the children used to get up in the morning and watch the Modern Farmer television program at 6 a.m. because it was the only program broadcasting at that hour. They also liked the "honky tonk" atmosphere of the midway. It reminded them of Coney Island.

At some point that summer, Genie the cat disappeared and they never did find her. Shortly after the Flemington Fair, they left Darts Mills and moved into a house at Larison's Corner near Ringoes, about five miles south of Flemington. Dot recalls, "We lived at Darts Mill just for the summer, as I recall from family mythology. My Dad was only on a short-term contract for the summer with the hospital, then Dr. Rannels decided to not come back and we stayed in New Jersey and moved to Ringoes (Larison's Corner) in the fall of 1958. David and Dick started school at East Amwell Township school."

Chapter 7

Larison's Corner
Making Hunterdon County their permanent home

Larison's Corner, like Darts Mills, is a local name given to a particular area that is not on a map.

Jerry had a friend from Cornell Medical Center, Sam Shapiro, whose mother and aunt owned a farm at Larison's Corner, a bit more than a half mile east of Route 31 off Old York Road. Shapiro had worked the farm in the early 1950s but then he later chose to go to medical school.

A lane runs several hundred yards south from Old York Road to the farm house, and there are two houses nearer the road that were rentals. The Barads rented the first house from 1958 until 1961. During that time the dairy farm was worked by the Shephard family who lived in the main farm house. The barn and the other farm buildings were farther down the lane past both houses. Frank and Helen Shephard had three daughters: Pat, Debbie and Kathy. Pat was a year or two older than David, Debbie was the same age as David and she became the first girl he developed a "crush" on, and Kathy (called Katie) was Dot's age.

Mr. Shephard and his father, who lived with them, always called David and Dick by the nickname "Doc" which bothered David because he was only seven years old and knew he wasn't a doctor. Mr. Shephard also had a bugle. When he played the bugle all the cows came running to see what was going on.

Two families lived in the other house on the property while the Barads lived there. For the first few years the house was occupied by the Bonds. Tray Bond was a year younger than David and a year older than Dick, and his sister Cynthia (called "Cyn") was Dot's age. Their mom, Thelma Bond, was from the south and hers was the first southern accent that David remembers hearing.

After the Bonds moved out, the second family to move in was named Feree. There were two Feree brothers: Steve, who was two years older than David, and Mike, who was Dick's age. They also had a sister Lisa who was the same age as Dot. Mr. Feree worked at the Bemis Bag Company near Flemington. Once he brought home a roll of plastic burlap and the kids ended up building a two-story frame out of scrap wood and covered it with burlap. It was called their "fort."

It was while they were living in Larison's Corner that Bob joined the family on April 25, 1959. Prior to his birth, the family held a meeting to decide on a name for the baby. Dot suggested "Alan" (even though she secretly wanted the baby to be a girl, so the siblings would be even: two boys and two girls), and that became his middle name.

"I remember Dad taking us to the medical center (Bob was the only Barad child born in the Hunterdon Medical Center) with our telescope," Dot remembered. "Children were not allowed in the maternity ward, even if it was my father's maternity ward. Mom held the baby up to the hospital window and the three of us got our first look at Bobby through our telescope Dad set up in the front lawn of the hospital."

The Barad house had very little hot water and it was always a struggle to have a warm bath. There was a grape arbor in the front yard with concord grapes, and Jerry tried making grape wine one year. Unfortunately, David closed the air release spigot on the cask and it blew up on the front porch.

David recalls, "Sometime when we lived in Ringoes, Dad assigned us to do household chores. At that time chores would be weeding the garden and of course taking care of the goats. Since I was older I was made de facto foreman, responsible to see that the chores got done. I was, of course, about eight years old at the time.

"On Saturday morning Dad would walk me around and tell me which rows in the vegetable garden needed to be weeded and then he would go to the hospital to see his patients. He generally came home by late morning and expected the morning chores to be done. My job was to enlist Dick and Dot (as she grew older) to help with the chores.

It was not easy to get Dick out of bed to do this. I got up, and woke him, and got dressed, and woke him again and again. Often, I would just start doing the work since it was easier than waking Dick up.

"I offered him choices … 'Do you want to set up the sprinkler or weed the lettuce...' making clear that staying in bed was not an option. Eventually I came up with the idea of the stampede.

"Stampedes were often part of the plot in the westerns on TV back then. In the TV shows the steers would all run together in one direction eventually knocking over the camera. I used this idea to get Dick out of bed. I stood next to his bed and started slowly running in place. When he became aware that I was making noise next to his bed I started running in place faster and louder. Eventually I ran very fast and loud in place and then called, 'Stampede!!' and jumped on top of him and kept moving my legs and arms like I was a charging steer. Eventually we wrestled to the floor and he would then get up. It became a joke between us and an excuse to rough house and wrestle around a bit.

"Much later, when we were both in high school, Dad still assigned us chores but it became harder and harder to get Dick to help. He was very serious about his homework, much more serious than I was. Often I ended up mowing the lawn or setting the sprinkler myself because Dick was still busy at his homework."

Dot remembers that David and Dick shared a room, "I did not walk into that room without knocking." She also recalled a story about hunting for the Lindbergh ransom treasure (they did not live too far from the Charles Lindbergh estate in nearby Hopewell, NJ, where the Lindbergh baby had been kidnapped), digging for it in the woods, but David remembered it was not the Lindbergh treasure they went hunting for, but that of the legend that John Ringo buried treasure from a train robbery there (see Sources).

The Moncriefs were neighbors who lived across a pasture to the east of the farm. Bill Moncrief was David's age and Bobby Moncrief was the same age as Dick. Mrs. Hillgardener was the kindergarten teacher that year in the East Amwell Township and Dickie and Bobby Moncrief were in her kindergarten class together. One day, for some reason, Bea sent Dot to school with Dickie and Bobby to visit their class. "The kids all thought I was so small," Dot recalled, "and they spent their whole recess picking me up to see how light I was." There was also something memorable about that class: "I remember there was a Tom (Humbles), Dick (Barad), and Harry (sorry, can't remember his last name)," Dot later recalled, which was memorable because a common expression of the 1950s referred to "every Tom, Dick, and Harry".

East Amwell School was small and each grade had only one

class. Other teachers at East Amwell were: Mrs. Denton (1st grade), Mrs. Bowe (2nd grade), Mrs. Curly (3rd grade), Mrs. Burns (4th grade), and Mrs. Coates (5th grade). The Barads moved to Delaware Township after David was in 5th grade, so Dick would not have gotten past Mrs. Curly. Mrs. Burns was the aunt of Edd "Kookie" Burns who starred on the television show *77 Sunset Strip* that ran from 1958 to 1964.

(For some first-hand accounting of how Dick and Bob Moncrief played as children, see Bob's account in Appendix P).

Jerry and "the boys" joined the YMCA father-son Indian Guides along with the Moncriefs. Each of the boys assumed an Indian name. Jerry's Indian name was "Saguaro" which meant "very tall cactus." Dick's name was "Peyote" (a cactus with hallucinogenic properties). David's Indian Guide name was Cholla (pronounced "Choia" which meant "jumping cactus"). Dot was not included but as with most family-oriented activities she tagged along. "Going away on weekend camping trips was fun," Dot remembers. "Dad taught us how to paddle a canoe. We had canoe races and spent time splashing each other's canoes with paddles. Once we explored a small creek that ran off the lake, and we felt like Lewis and Clark."

Scratchy made it to Larison's Corner and had several litters of kittens there. One group of new kittens once followed David, Dick, and Dot across the field as they walked to see Billy and Bobby Moncrief. Unfortunately, the Moncrief's neighbor had some dogs. When the kids crossed that lawn with the seven or eight kittens following, the dogs came running out and chased the kittens. None of the kittens survived the encounter and the children were horrified. It was their first personal experience of death and Dot remembers all of them crying for much of the day.

Another family that lived nearby was the Zengs. The Zeng farm was south of the Barads across a couple of fields and up a small incline. There was a road that ran between the pastures south of the barn all the way to the Zeng's. Bill Zeng and his wife had seven children including Billy, the oldest, Bobby who was a year older than David, and Lisa who was Dick's age and maybe his first "girlfriend."

The Zengs had a ram that stayed on the front lawn and would butt anyone who attempted to cross. They also had at least one

horse (which was featured in several Barad family pictures), and a
bull steer that was kept in the barn yard. Mr. Zeng told the children
to be careful of the bull. One morning when Dick, Dot, and Lisa
were walking across one of the fields, they didn't realize that the
bull was in that field. Suddenly, the bull started to chase the three
kids who ran as quickly as they could to the nearest fence. Dick
and then Dot managed to get over the fence but somehow Lisa
couldn't climb or slipped trying to and was left on the other side of
the fence with the bull rapidly closing in. Dick didn't hesitate: he
leaned way over the fence, grabbed Lisa by the shirt and pulled her
over the fence and the two tumbled into a pile on the ground. The
bull stopped. It was a real scary moment; so much so that the three
didn't tell the adults because they were afraid that Mr. Zeng would
have been angry at them for being in that field and they didn't want
to get into trouble. But Lisa kept telling Dick how he saved her
life.

Mr. Zeng was an airline pilot with Eastern Airlines and he flew
often out of Newark Airport. David remembers Mr. Zeng's study
in the house contained many airplane artifacts in it. Once Mr. Zeng
arranged for the boys' Cub Scout troop to visit the air traffic
control tower at Newark Airport, and David remembers being
impressed with all the radar screens and lights in the tower.

Mr. Zeng died when his plane crashed near Lake Pontchartrain
just north of New Orleans in 1964 shortly after takeoff (see
Sources). He was only 47 years old. Dot and David both recall how
sad it was when Bea and Jerry took their children over to the Zeng
house to pay their respects.

To the west of their house was an orchard of apple, pear, and
plum trees, and the falling fruit was a favorite for ground hornets.
There were many yellow jacket nests in the orchard and walking in
there was like walking in a minefield. Jerry tried to mow the
orchard with his rotary mower and when he crossed a hornets'
nest, the hornets flew up in a cloud like in a cartoon. Anyone in the
area would run for cover into the house.

The perimeter of the orchard was surrounded by old chicken
sheds. One was a large two-story structure. The floors of these
sheds were covered in old chicken droppings with thousands of
meal worms feeding below. The children used to collect the meal
worms to feed to their pet lizards, snakes, and turtles. They had a

turtle pit in the back yard with half a dozen box turtles and a few painted turtles that Jerry collected whenever he saw them crossing the roads. They also had a large fish tank in Jerry's study that housed a variety of reptiles at various times, including an iguana, small Cayman alligators, and snakes. The reptiles were supposed to be Dick's.

One summer Dick and David and their neighbor Tray Bond took a door from one of the old chicken houses and wedged it onto a branch in the biggest apple tree to make the platform of a tree house. Ultimately, there were three platforms in that tree on different levels and a ladder nailed to the trunk.

Jerry had some old canvas tents, and some evenings all the neighbor kids camped out in the orchard, including the Shephard girls. They lit a campfire, toasted marshmallows, sang songs, told ghost stories, and ultimately slept in the tents.

There was considerable sunspot activity in the late 1950s and consequently the Aurora Borealis was visible in the night sky. Of course, there was less light pollution then, too, and it was easy to see the Milky Way. Sometimes the kids would lie on their backs at night in August and watch shooting stars. Jerry bought them a refracting telescope that allowed them to look at the moons of Jupiter, the rings of Saturn, and, of course, the Moon. They also had a special filter that allowed them to look at the sun spots, too.

The Barads were living at Larison's Corner on October 4, 1957, when the first Russian satellite, Sputnik, was launched. David and Dot remember watching some satellites streak across the evening sky during the years they lived there but David doubts that they could see Sputnik.

The kids remember lots of snow back then, in the late 1950s. The drifts rose up the sides of the house, and the snow was so deep it covered the parked cars. One winter, they were snowed in for a week. Jerry invited strangers who were stuck on the road in front of the house to stay with them.

The Barads kept goats and ducks on the farm. Dick and David joined 4H and went to the Flemington Fair to participate in the 4H Goat Show. Some animal got into the shed on the farm and masticated the ducks so they did not last long.

Dick and David accompanied Jerry to a Cactus and Succulent convention in St Louis in 1959. While they were there they did two great things: they visited the Meramec Caverns, the largest commercial cave in the state of Missouri (the legend was that Jessie James had a hideout there), and they brought back a suitcase full of fireworks, which were illegal to purchase in New Jersey. From then on Fourth of July was celebrated with fireworks, mostly Roman candles and bottle rockets. The kids used to put firecrackers in apples and throw them in the air to watch them explode. With the Ferees, they made a "cannon" out of a pipe and mounted it on a wagon. They would then drop lit firecrackers in it and shoot at the windows in the old chicken house.

The chicken houses all had slanted roofs. The kids climbed onto the roof and dared each other to jump from higher and higher points. Dick once jumped off and his chin landed on his knee and he bit through his tongue creating a pretty bloody scene.

There was also a hand-pumped well behind the first house where the Ferees and Bonds lived. This was base for a summer game called "Midnight Starlight," a night time game of hide and seek. During the summer, they played until 10 p.m. almost every night. Once Dot hid in a Boxwood tree at the front of the house. No one found her. Steve Feree was "it" and he later asked her where she had hidden. She showed him the tree. The next night, Steve tried to hide in the same tree, but he was bigger and he hit a wasp's nest and got stung. Jerry Barad killed all the wasps but thought that the nest was so beautifully built that he brought it inside the house and kept it.

Dick smashed his thumb one time under the cement pump cover so badly that a tendon was exposed and Jerry had to run him into the emergency room at the hospital to get it stitched up. David remembers Dick as not being so much accident-prone but that if one of the three of them was going to get hurt, it would probably be Dick. (Although David did recall one time when he got run over by the wagon cart being pulled by Jerry on his tractor.)

Dot remembers: "I hated peas... and so did Dick... I think we called the peas 'golf balls' cause they would pucker up and look like a golf ball. One night in the late 1950s, Dick and I were left at the table and David was excused to watch TV. Maybe it was the Disney show. Anyway, Dick and I were pretty agitated at being left at the table but not enough to down those yucky peas. We got into a fight and I punched him in the arm without realizing I had my fork in my hand. I stuck him with the fork. My, was that a big surprise for both of us!

"Years later: I was working at the Hunterdon Medical Center one summer and Dick was working in the HMC Lab learning to draw blood. He called me at lunch time to come meet him for lunch, and when I showed up he had a big smile on his face. He had been practicing with the needle on oranges all morning but it was time to try on a real person. He remembered I owed him one stick from the fork incident of our youth and who was I to deny him? By the way, he did it perfectly: pulled several tubes of blood not losing any suction. A natural born blood sucker."

Dot also remembered something that Dick started with her that continued his entire life: "One day when we were kids in elementary school, Dick asked me if I had a good memory. I said I did. He said he wanted to test me and he was going to tell me a number and from now on if he had asked me to remember something I was to say this number. 'Okay,' I said. 'So what's the number?' He looked real serious for a moment and said, 'Three. Can you remember that?' 'Sure,' I said. So, over the years when I would least expect it he would randomly say, 'Hey, didn't I ask you to remember something?' I would immediately respond with, 'Three!' And then the conversation just continued. This never did stop."

Chapter 8

Delaware Township
The old house on the new property

Dot recalls: "We moved to the 'old house' from Ringoes in 1961. I was in second grade which put Dick in 4th. Mann was his teacher. I had her, too. Dick's best friends at the time were Bennet Waugh and Gary Bronsveld. With the arrival of the Beatles in 1963, my brother decided to learn to play guitar.

"The 'old house' refers to an old farm house on the property that Jerry and Bea bought on Route 523 west of Flemington, in Delaware Township. There is a very long driveway leading back to the property, a wide expanse of about twenty acres that used to be a working farm. We moved into the old farmhouse while the new house was being built and we thought we would be able to move in by the end of the summer. The house wasn't completed until January 1 when dad used the tractor and a hay wagon to move our stuff from one house to the other. The new house was at the end of the driveway that would also be at the top of the hill, providing a beautiful vista."

There are two other houses to drive past along the driveway to get to the Barads. "The Pebbles built and lived in the first house when we moved to the farm," Dot explains. "The Strobers built and lived in the second house that the Fishkins now live in. The Strobers made more of an impression on us as Irwin Strober and his wife June were very young. Mr. Strober had a bunch of brothers and they all worked for the family business, which is a roofing company. They had four small children with Toby being the oldest, and he was three years younger than I was. Jerry Strober was Bobby's age. The others were all too small to make an impression on me."

To help entertain his young brood, Irwin Strober built his house around two bowling alleys, mostly because he had such young children. They also had a pool table, a jukebox for music, and pinball machines. This way his brothers and friends could come over and party in the basement but not need to leave the kids home with a babysitter. Many Friday and Saturday nights would find a lot of people over at the Strobers for fun. The bowling alley was only semi-automatic, so the Barad children were asked to come over to set pins for the night, and were paid a dollar a night.

"This was a lot of fun as there was popular music on the juke box and I imagine they were drinking beer but I do not remember that," Dot recalled. "These weren't the kind of people my parents hung out with so this made a big impression on us. Maybe too much of an impression as I believe my mom decided it wasn't a good idea for us to hang around there."

Frank Schneider, a famous stock car driver in the area, lived across the road from the Barad's driveway, but the Barad boys were never much interested in cars at the time.

"We had to walk every day to catch the bus at the top of the driveway along Route 523," Dot remembers. "We stood for the bus every morning with Frankie's kids. If the bus was coming around the corner and we were not yet at the top of our lane, Frankie's kids had a screeching signal they used to let us know to run.

"Dick played Little League baseball. He was a big baseball fan. He loved Sandy Koufax and was very proud of him as a baseball player who was Jewish. We Jews are many things but outstanding athletes were very uncommon.

"Of course, everyone felt ripped off when the Brooklyn Dodgers moved to LA, so in the end Dick became a Yankees fan. When Dick and Nancy were at Albert Einstein College of Medicine, they also had season tickets to see the Yankees. I remember going with them for a game. It was sunset and the sound system was blaring out the Bee Gee's *Staying Alive* from 'Saturday Night Fever'. It was beautiful."

Koufax is remembered as one of the outstanding Jewish athletes in American sports. His decision to not pitch Game 1 of the 1965 World Series because it fell on Yom Kippur garnered national attention as an example of conflict between social pressures and personal beliefs.

Another family that became friends with the Barads were the Motz family, and this would have a lasting impact on Dick during his senior year in high school. Oldest son Randy Motz was in David's class and his younger sister Pam was in Dick's. The Motz family lived in Raritan Township, about five miles from the Barads, but friendships between the kids developed quickly, and were soon cemented. Pam Motz remembers that Dick was her first date when he took her to a Scout dance on December 19, 1964.

Randy remembers: "Though we did not live in the same neighborhood, the Barad family and our family were extremely close friends. We spent a lot of time at their home and participated in family events like the boy's bar mitzvahs, and Dorothy's wedding. There were terrorizing sled rides down the hill and into the woods in back of their home in the winter and pool parties in the summer. Some of the most memorable times of my early years were spent at their house.

"When the Beatles initially took the U.S. by storm, of course every musician wanted to mimic them. David, Dick and I were no different. At that point none of us were accomplished musicians or vocalists but we were going to give it a try. Mrs. Barad planned a party for one of the kids, I do not remember which one at this point, and invited a whole bunch of friends from our school. We decided to entertain them with our take-off on the Beatles.

"David and Dick had guitars, but I did not have drums, so we fabricated a set out of wood, cardboard, and anything else we could get our hands on. At one point during the party, we performed a karaoke version of several popular Beatles tunes. Looking back on it now, it was pretty hokey, but at the time it rocked and everyone thought we were so cool."

But it would be the influence of things and people who were British that would cast the two families closer together than any of them could have imagined.

Randy mentioned the sledding during the winter. The sled run at the Barad's house was of epic proportions. Fifty years later, whenever I contacted someone about this book project, if they had ever been sledding at the Barad's, they would still mention the sled run.

Dot described it: "Sledding on Christmas. When we grew up, that was the favorite. The great sled path we had at the house had multiple runs, with banks and jumps and tunnels. We built it every year and dug it out after each snow. It was a whole neighborhood project. It ran from the top of my parents' cement steps past the now swimming pool/then greenhouse, past the barn, down the field toward the pond.

"There it split into three parts, each part with its own bank and jumps and tunnels. At the point where there is a fence now, the paths all came together into one very large long bank. Then it shot you through the woods where you had to get through a bunch of trees ending in a jump which on a good year ended on open ice on a frozen pond. The worst thing was walking back up the hill. The best thing was sledding at night by a full moon and all the stars."

David described one particular sled race between he, Dick, Randy Motz, and another friend, Fred Huber:

"The 40-second Sled Run" – as remembered by David Barad

Cold snow biting my face. A breeze blows up the hill. Pull the wool down farther over my ears.
Hold the sled. A hand on each side rail.
The sun is low over the trees and the clouds to the west look yellow and purple and pink.
The snow with twinkles of light, sparkle like sequins.
Dick is walking up the hill. His boots crunch the ice topping the 14 inches of snow. As he steps the snow first seems to support him --- and then "crunch" it gives way and he sinks down.

This is a race. Four of us will compete. The top of the sled path is funneled out to accommodate up to six simultaneous sleds but 25 feet below only two sleds can fit on the path at a time.

Randy is to my right and Fred to my left. Dick takes his position to the right of Randy.

"On your mark, get set, go."
I run a few steps and ease my Flexible Flyer onto the path.

My right gloved hand brushes against the bank of ice and snow on my right as I move ahead of Fred.

"Shhhhhhhh... tss...shhhh" the runners grip the ice on the path.
Randy has beaten me into the shoot. His boots are inches in front of my face.
"Shhhh...tsssssss....kkh tisss... "Randy hits the left bank and slows

and my sled moves ahead and taps the back of his boots. We are approaching the first banked turn.

Randy's sled slides sideways across the ice kicking up a soft spray of crystals, but he must drag his left foot to maintain control and to force an acute left turn. I opt to move above him on the bank to his right. He has slowed enough that we are now parallel. As I come down off the turn I run into the right side of his sled.

"Cach cunk ugh ..." the sleds are momentarily locked together as we are bearing fast down on the snow tunnel. The tunnel fits only one sled. Dick comes up behind me and pushes my left boot with his hand as my sled veers to the right of the tunnel. Randy runs through the tunnel followed by Dick and then Fred.

My sled is crunching into the ice and snow on the right bank next to the tunnel. I get up and relaunch onto the path.

All four sleds take the second turn and bear to the right down the steepest part of the hill as we all four pick up speed and finally leap into the air at the bottom of the hill as the path ends at an embankment.

" KKK-Comph.." the sleds hit the bottom and all four are slowing. The water of the pond is coming up ahead and it is not frozen completely. We run into the reeds at the edge and roll off the sleds onto our backs, each one of us panting steam.

"Ready to go again?" someone shouts. And we all get up and race up the hill.

Perfect...

The back porch and steps of the Barad home.

Chapter 9

Hunterdon Central High School
The high school we called "home"

Hunterdon Central Regional High School is situated north of Flemington on the east side of, and facing, Route 31. In a statewide effort to regionalize local high schools into more central locations in the 1950s, four such high schools were established in Hunterdon County. North Hunterdon (known simply as "North") is the northern most school, located on Route 31 in Annandale, about 8 miles north of Flemington. "Central" is in Raritan Township, which surrounds the town of Flemington. "South" is situated just outside of Lambertville about 10 miles south of Flemington. Delaware Valley, or "Del Val," is in the western more rural areas of the county, closer to the Delaware River.

Central was the sending school for Raritan Township, Readington Township, and parts of East Amwell Township and Delaware Township. At the time it opened in 1958, it had only one building and there had been a controversy about how big the auditorium should be. Many people thought that a 600-seat auditorium would be big enough. But Board of Education Vice President William J. Layden, among others, disagreed. Convinced that this school would grow and expand in the coming years, Layden fought for, and won, the construction of a 1,000-seat auditorium.

Ten years later, when David Barad's class graduated, they couldn't fit all of the parents and family of the graduating students into the auditorium at the same time.

The school mascot, "Red Devils," was also controversial. Many times over the years a parent approached the Board of Education to complain about the "evil" mascot name. The complainants never prevailed, and HCHS students are still known as the Red Devils to this day.

Dick played guitar and French horn while in high school. During football season, he played the French horn in the marching band during the pre-game and half time shows. He also played in the concert band, and he played guitar in the pit bands for the high

43

school musicals.

Near the end of our junior year (1969), Dick ran for President of the Student Council for the term that would run during our senior year, and he won. Now, in many high schools, the Student Council is mostly a formality. It sends a representative to some Board of Education meetings, it holds meetings about concerns in the high school and then forwards those concerns to the building principal, and that's about it. It looks good on the college application to be able to say "Student Council President," even if you hadn't done anything.

But Dick was not like that.

He was an activist during the end of the 1960s, when activism was considered a bad thing by many people. But his activism had deep family roots.

Great-great grandparents, Nathan and Leah Barad, were Russian Jews who spoke Yiddish and had firsthand experience with the violent pogroms against the Jews in Odessa. The family hung a cross on their front door to escape from harm. It is not known if the family observed Jewish traditions and holidays, but it is known that their son David Nathan Barad was a socialist who rejected religion.

While a student at the university, David met fellow student and future wife Adele Leventon. He eventually earned a Ph.D. degree in Chemistry from the University of Zurich (his degree hangs on great-grandson David's wall) and he also attended the University in Kiev. He emigrated to the United States in 1892 after meeting an American who promised him a job as a chemist in Cleveland, but that turned out not to be true. Not knowing how to speak English, David's first job in America was to be a "barker" outside of a market in a Jewish neighborhood of Cleveland where he would entice fellow Jews in Yiddish to shop at the market. Adele joined him there in 1894 and they were married right away.

He found work in his field in Philadelphia, and he and Adele moved there. Their first child, a daughter they named Victoria, was born on February 2, 1895. Family history says that David became a chemist for the DuPont Company and eventually became supervisor of the dye preparation department, and that it was his dye formula that created the green color used in U.S. paper currency.

Adele was homesick, so when David was invited back to Russia in 1897 to deliver a paper at his old university, they accepted the invitation, even though Adele was very pregnant. Upon their arrival on Russian soil, David was jailed for "revolutionary" political activities he had been involved in at the university about 10 years earlier. In one of the earliest recorded instances of his use of dyes, he had printed anti-government posters while he was a university student, something of the kind his mother Leah had suspected when he came home with ink-stained hands.

While he was in jail, Adele was likely staying with her in-laws. She gave birth to their second child, a son they named Alexander, on June 10, 1897. Since his parents were naturalized American citizens, Alexander was a United States citizen when he was born in Russia. Conflicting reports exist about David's ultimate release from jail: either the DuPont Company was instrumental in getting David released from prison, or his mother was able to either pull some strings or "grease some palms," or possibly both.

The family soon returned to the United States and would never again see Russia, but Adele always thought fondly of her childhood home, keeping an etching of her homeland on one of her walls.

Just over 100 years after his great-grandfather David was born, Dick Barad took up his family tradition of activism as a high school student. If there was a cause, Dick got involved. And as Student Council President, he got the Student Council involved as well.

In the fall of 1969, when we had just become seniors at HCHS, the voting age in New Jersey was 21. A referendum appeared on the general election ballot that November 4 to lower the voting age to 18. Dick thought that that was the right thing to do, so he, and the Council, got involved. More than 70 students from Central became activists the weekend before the election. They took 10,000 flyers that had been provided by The Voting Age Coalition in Trenton and distributed them in parking lots and at the football game that weekend in support of the lowering of the voting age.

Dick also took out an ad, in the name of the Student Council but obviously written by himself, in the local weekly newspaper, The Hunterdon County Democrat (see Appendix D). The newspaper was owned by Republicans and, as was stated on the front page of each week's edition, the newspaper was "not affiliated with any political party." On behalf of the HCHS Student Council, the ad urged voters to vote in favor of lowering the voting age.

In the ad, he appealed to the present voters in the county and state to vote in favor of the referendum to give those 18-20-year-olds the right to vote "by asking for a chance to prove our honest concern and maturity."

Dick also wrote a Letter to the Editor of The Democrat that was printed shortly before the referendum vote urging the voters "to trust the youth of our state" by voting to lower the voting age. "The 'magic' of the number 21," he wrote, "comes straight from the Middle Ages. A man of that age could fight and own land" and, thus, was given the right to vote at that age. Dick went on to point out that even though the Renaissance brought about societal changes around the world, "the 'magic' of the age 21 is still with us." He pointed out that "(T)oday's youth are the involved generation" and that young men 18 and older were in the military, yet they were inexplicably denied the right to vote and "should have some say in the affairs of the country for which they fight and die" (to read the complete letter, see Appendix E).

To no avail. The referendum was defeated by a 6-4 margin: 13,188 against to 8,319 in favor.

As reported in the Democrat in a story following the election, Dick had "argued that being part of the television age and a revolutionary society has brought about a deep realization of national and international affairs at an early age" and that there was a "genuine concern and belief in the nation and that the young had hoped to gain public support 'not by loud demands and senseless riots but by an organized plea for public support'."

The fact that it didn't happen in 1969 didn't deter Dick. He was also quoted in the same newspaper article, "If it goes on the ballot next time, I'll be working for it."

Such was the tenacity and foresight of Dick Barad. However, his help wasn't needed. On April 3, 1971, the New Jersey legislature ratified the 26th amendment to the US Constitution granting voting privileges to those 18 and older.

Music was also an important part of Dick's life, even in high school. Randy Motz remembered: "In high school, Dave, Dick, myself (I played bass) and Danny Vlahakis on drums started a band called The Rainn (yes, with two 'Ns'). We thought we were pretty good at the time but did not really stick with it. We were all interested in so many other activities that dedicating ourselves to being in a band was just not in the cards.

"We did play at a high school dance and I remember we played in a school talent show ("The Devil's Cabaret", 1968) in front of hundreds of our classmates and parents. We played a song called 'Windy' by The Association and it came out pretty good, though none of us had the vocal skills to pull off the incredible harmonies that were required. It was not long after this performance that the band broke up. Dick was a good guitar player but I remember that he was not very comfortable performing in front of people."

In the summer of 1969, David remembers, he attended folk music festivals with some of his friends in Newport, Rhode Island, and in Philadelphia. Dick did not go to these with him, David remembers, but there was one festival that Dick did not want to miss: Woodstock.

"It as Dick's idea, and I said 'Okay'," David remembered. The two of them drove up to the Woodstock festival in Bethel, New York, on a Friday afternoon, arriving in the Catskill Mountains off the New York Thruway and, along with some others looking for a place to spend the night, made their way into a boarded-up hotel to spend Friday night. The next morning, with tickets in hand, they walked to Yasgur's farm, meeting a girl David had met at the Newport Folk Festival a few weeks earlier.

"That was funny because among 50,000 people, you run into someone you know," David recalled.

When they arrived at the site, there was no one to collect their tickets (which David still has), so they made their way about three quarters of the way up the hill, off to the left of the stage, found a spot and sat down to listen to the music.

"I don't remember the music that much. I mean there certainly were a lot of people smoking dope and doing acid," David said. "Every now and then some spaced-out guy would go running by and somebody naked would go running by but we were mostly trying to listen to the music."

They didn't have any food, and towards nightfall they realized that they hadn't brought any sleeping bags, either. "It was mostly cold," David said. "We kind of huddled together there on the hill, kind of spooned. There were some other people there and we were all kind of spooning together just to be warm. Then it rained a bit.

"They played all night, all the way until the morning. I think I fell asleep first. I think Dick heard The Who but I didn't hear the introduction of 'Tommy' which was the first time they ever played that song. When I woke up, Sly and the Family Stone and Janis Joplin were singing."

Finally, sometime on Sunday morning, realizing they were wet, cold, and hungry, they decided not to stay through until the end of the festival. They walked within 15 feet of the stage as they made their way down the hill, through the mud, and out of the farm.

"Dick was very proud of having gone to Woodstock," said David, "and I remember when the movie came out, which seemed like forever but was only a year or two later, he was really gung ho that we should go see it. I think it had more philosophical weight for him. I don't know. It seemed to move him more. And of course, I appreciate it as a memory of him."

And as they were leaving Woodstock, even though they didn't know it, a jet plane was passing over their heads, headed for a New York airport from London, England. Among the passengers was a petite brunette named Jackie Herbert, who was about to have a profound impact on Dick's life.

Chapter 10

Jackie
The British Invasion

Jacqueline Ann Herbert was a beautiful, demure brunette from England who would spend the 1969-1970 school year at Hunterdon Central as part of a student exchange program sponsored by the American Field Service (AFS). She lived for the year with the Motz family in Raritan Township. She was the same age as Pam Motz and would be a senior at Hunterdon Central. Pam and Jackie became fast friends. One of the first people Pam introduced Jackie to was Dick Barad. It was Fate.

In 1968, 17-year-old Jackie was studying two of her favorite subjects – British Literature and History of Art – in her hometown of Sutton Coldfield, England. She was at the crossroads that most juniors in high school face: where to go to college, and "how will the two subjects I love most offer me a career"? She couldn't decide on a path for either question, and was procrastinating making any kind of decision when a notice was posted at her school inviting students to apply for a year of study as an "exchange student" in America.

Unsure of her future in England, she "jumped at the chance."

The program was sponsored by the AFS, an international exchange program originally set up by British and American ambulance crews during the world wars. Since soldiers from different countries developed friendships on the battlefield that survived into and flourished in peacetime, the program was established to allow young people, the leaders of the future, an opportunity to experience the cultures of other countries.

According to Jackie, "it was hoped that the friendships created would promote peace and consequently the possibility of conflict between countries would be less likely."

The AFS selection process was rigid, accepting only students with at least a B average, and the successful completion of a series of interviews. Jackie survived both, and in the spring of 1969 she received her letter of acceptance.

With the heartfelt and financial support of her parents, who had attended each of the interviews with her, Jackie prepared as best she could for a year away from home. She would be in a different country, living with people she did not know, and attending a completely different type of high school for her senior year. Communications with those back home were limited to mostly letters, since trans-Atlantic telephone calls were very expensive.

By August, 1969, she and 50 other British student ambassadors were flying into U.S. airspace when the flight captain came on to the loudspeaker system to inform his passengers that that big group of people assembled below them were attending a music festival known as "Woodstock." Welcome to America.

Jackie flew into JFK airport in New York, and she and the other students spent several days at Hofstra University on Long Island until the host families could come get them. They had exchanged letters and photos for several weeks prior, and the Motz family – dad Ralph, his wife Dot, oldest son Randy, daughter Pam, and youngest son Brian – came and brought Jackie back to the Flemington area.

"The next day," Jackie recalled, "Dot Motz had arranged for us all to visit friends called the Barads for something called Brunch. As it turned out, I liked both things a lot."

The Barad household was something quite different from anything or anyone Jackie had met before. "I remember that the family seemed so outgoing and confident," Jackie recalled. "I was at that time pretty shy and spent a lot of time pretending not to be, so the onslaught of so many confident people in one place was something to get used to."

She was introduced to Bea who was in the midst of making "vast amounts of French toast and bacon" for everyone. "Bea was an amazing woman," said Jackie, "and I was charmed from the first. She welcomed me warmly."

When she met Jerry, she could see right away how the Barad family dynamic worked. "When Jerry came home from work, he would grab whichever of his kids was passing at the time and they would disappear into a great bear hug of affection. It was attractive to see a family who seemed so at ease," Jackie recalled.

She also met Dot, "who was simply beautiful. With her big smile, clouds of hair and willowy figure, she was lovely. A year younger than me and still a girl really. I liked her straight away."

David, who by then was in college, and his girlfriend and soon-to-be wife Iris were also there. "They looked happy and good together," Jackie remembered. "Because David was in college he seemed very grown up. A couple of years seemed like a lot then." Bob Barad, however, "was only about 11 when I first met him. A boy with a mop of dark hair and big spectacles, he was at the mercy of his siblings' endless teasing and was frustrated at not being old enough to be included in everything that David, Dick, and Dot and their friends were up to."

And then she met Dick. "There was so much going on that morning and so much to take in, but Dick was a naturally memorable person," Jackie recalled. "I suppose my first impression was of a good-looking boy with a great smile and an easy manner dressed in blue jeans and an open neck shirt. He was taller than me and had a mass of dark curly hair brushed into submission from a side parting. The most striking feature about him, though, were his eyes which seemed to literally sparkle. Dick's eyes were always full of life. Whatever he was doing, they just pulled you in.

"Even that first day," she admitted, "I saw what fun he was to be with. He would crease up with laughter, jostle with his friends and family and fool about. From the beginning, I learned, too, that Dick and his friends were not just lightweights: they took political issues seriously, they cared about social justice, environmental change, and the possibility of change. I admired the commitment shown by my new friends and especially admired Dick and his ambition to make a difference and do his best in the world. I had never been exposed to that kind of awareness before in my own peer group at home, so this was really interesting to me."

Dick had set his sights on getting accepted into Cornell University, as his father had done, and that fall he continued his pattern of commitment to his studies, as well as leading an activist Student Council, and participating in marching band (which meant practices every day after school and performances every Saturday at the football games). Jackie became a very popular addition to the HCHS Class of 1970, but there was one thing that frustrated her. "While I admired all that he did," she remembered, "it nearly drove me mad that he seemed to have no time for anything else, especially not a girlfriend."

In the fall, after football season ended on Thanksgiving Day, the marching band sponsored what was called a Military Ball, a very formal dance with tuxedos and gowns. Jackie was asked to the Ball by many different boys but she gracefully declined each invitation. "I was being asked to the Ball and was turning down potential escorts in the vain hope that Dick would ask me," she recalled. Eventually he did ask her "and we had a great time," she remembered. "Unfortunately, on the way home, the car stopped dead and we realized that he had forgotten to fill the car with petrol so that we ended up having to walk half a mile back to his house in deep snow, me wearing an evening dress. Dick was embarrassed but we pretty soon saw the funny side and I was perfectly OK. So, laughing and shivering, we trudged our way back home. Bea was waiting and gave him a very hard time for making me walk in snow on such a cold night!"

Dick and Jackie became an "item" at school that year. They probably should have been voted the "class couple" that year since they were both so well-liked, but that designation went instead to George Buck and Linda Brumbaugh who had been dating since junior high. But Dick and Jackie became "DickandJackie" during 1969-70.

In Jackie's words: "Some people might remember the local telephone company in Flemington setting up a surprise link with my parents and brother to spring on me during my first, and most terrifying, talk to the school about what it was like to be an Exchange student. I couldn't have been more surprised, nor were my parents who just happened to be at home when the call went through. The subsequent conversation was amplified to the entire audience in the school auditorium and I well remember my extreme embarrassment as my mother asked "How is Dickie?" All eyes went to Dick who was sliding lower and lower into his chair in a useless effort to disappear altogether. It's amazing he ever spoke to me again."

Jackie fully enjoyed her year at Hunterdon Central. Dick was, in her words, "infuriatingly disciplined about studying and work" but Jackie also had obligations that kept the couple apart from time to time. One of those obligations was the AFS mandate that called for monthly weekend gatherings of the AFS students at different host homes within 100 miles or so. Jackie gladly attended and made new friends there as well. This also included a final two-week tour of the eastern U.S. before all the AFS students departed for home.

"It suddenly struck both Dick and I that my departure was imminent. For me it was terrible to leave, and he, too, was feeling pretty rotten about it. We didn't know if we would see each other again. We did have a chance to meet before I got onto the plane home but then I had to go. The song *Leaving on a Jet Plane* rang in our ears."

Before Jackie returned to England, the Barads hosted a farewell party at their home. I went because Jackie had become a very good friend of mine that year and I knew I was going to miss her, as did everyone there. When I hugged her and said goodbye, I didn't know if I would ever see her again. That was June, 1970. It was 42 years before I saw her again.

I wrote to Jackie at least once that I recall when I was a student at Jacksonville (Florida) University in 1970-71, but then I lost track of her until 2010 when we were planning the 40th HCHS reunion. She sent me an email picture of herself that I had enlarged and set on an easel at the reunion, and several classmates signed it. I mailed it to her to let her know that she was still a part of our class, and we all still missed her very much.

Jackie, Dick, Bob, and Dot (circa 1971)

Chapter 11

Cornell University
The Beginning of the Higher Education

After graduating from high school, the summer of 1970 held two big events in Dick's life: Jackie had to return to England, and then David and Dick took a two-week trip up the California Coastal Highway from Los Angeles to Oregon.

Dick had read an article in *Time* magazine about people driving up Highway 1, the Coast Highway in California, so he and David decided they were going to do the same. Along with Fred Huber and David Urbach, they flew to Los Angeles, rented a motor coach they could drive and live in, and drove all the way up the Coast Highway to Oregon. Stops along the way included Mendocino, California, and a commune.

As David tells it, "We put the camper on a beach. It was deserted when we got there and when we got up in the morning there were trucks all over the place... not trucks but little vehicles, and they were serving breakfast and they were filming a movie. There was this woman and she came out of the grocery store and she dropped her bags and the boy picked up the bags and handed them to her, and they would do it over again. They did it about 30 times. They were filming *The Summer of '42*. Of course, we didn't know who any of those people were."

David also remembered that along the way, Dick wasn't scared of climbing, and he scurried up little cliffs with no problems. They stopped in San Francisco and parked the camper down by Fisherman's Wharf, then drove on up to Mount Shasta in Oregon.

"We did go to one of those diners where they wouldn't let us in because it said 'No hippies' on the door," David recalled. "We ended up going to a commune where we stayed for a couple of days. We went swimming in a lake that was a glacial stream and it was very, very cold. So that was our California trip."

And then it was off to Ithaca, New York.

Dick's roommate during his freshman year at Cornell was his high school friend, Bill Johnson, from Flemington. Both Dick and

Bill were "legacy" students – those who had a parent who had graduated from Cornell. Bill's father conducted the interview with Dick, which didn't hurt Dick's chances for acceptance.

In an interview for this book in 2011, Bill Johnson still vividly remembered sledding in winter at the Barad's house as kids. While they were at Cornell in the early 1970s, "it was the end of the hippie era," Bill remembered, "except for Dick. He was a very straight arrow. I never knew him to do any kind of drugs or even drink alcohol. He was extremely dedicated as a student and focused on doing well. He was single-minded, and it was not uncommon for him to stay in the library studying until 10:30 at night."

Bill admitted that he was "in awe" of Dick's ability to stay focused on his studies. "There were a lot of 'stoners' at Cornell back then" but they had no influence on Dick, he recalled. The two Hunterdon boys both played guitar and on occasion they "jammed" together.

Bill's girlfriend from New Jersey, BJ, was also a frequent visitor to the Cornell campus where she stayed with Bill and Dick in their dorm room. "Dick was not always happy [about the amount of time BJ spent there] but he was generous with his time," Bill recalled.

Bill and BJ were classmates in the HCHS class of 1970 and had been dating for well over a year at the time of our graduation. BJ's father had been dying of cancer most of her senior year in high school and so there had not been a lot of thought by anyone in her family, including BJ, of what she would do after high school. Any plans about her going to college herself were put on hold. Her favorite uncle died at about the time of our graduation from HCHS, and exactly one month later, her father passed away.

"My family was in a shambles," she recalled, "and my boyfriend and all my friends--my entire support system--had gone to college." So, in the fall, adrift and virtually alone in New Jersey, BJ found her way to visit Bill at Cornell, and ended up staying.

In fact, Dick, Bill, and BJ had been good friends at HCHS. "Dick was a generous and patient and loving friend," BJ recalled. "He listened well and with compassion to me and seemed to understand how alone and adrift I felt. We often talked and he reflected without judgment on the things I said. He wanted more for me, and he was a friend to me at a time when I had no friends, and that meant more to me than I can ever say. I loved him for that."

There was one incident that Bill recalled that reflected several sides of Dick at the same time: his sense of adventure, his love of music, and the inability for others to influence his behavior.

"Dick and I hitchhiked one time 25 miles from Ithaca to Cortland, New York, to see a Grateful Dead concert," Bill said. At one point, they were given a ride by other concert-goers in a VW microbus. "Some of the passengers in the back of the van were passing around a bottle of Ripple wine, and before I took a drink, they told me it was 'electric Ripple' ...meaning that it was laced with LSD." While Bill drank some of the altered wine, Dick did not. "He was appalled," said Bill, but Dick served as Bill's "guiding spirit" that night, looking out for his friend and keeping him safe.

Michael Zweig met Dick a few days into their freshman year at Cornell on the same floor of Clara Dickson Hall. Zweig lived in a single room, just a few doors down from Dick and Bill.

Michael also recalled that Dick spent most of his time in the library, studying. "He was pre-med, and studied more intently and with more focus than any of us, and we studied a lot, to be sure, typically at least from 7 to 12 midnight, when the library finally closed. All of us, to some degree, experienced our freshman year from Dick's vantage point."

But it was not all studying, all the time. After studying (and sometimes before, and during) the guitars would fly out, and a guitar jam session between Bill and Dick would happen. Songs of the day, BJ singing along, Bill providing a joint if anyone wanted one. "Their room," Michael remembered, became "truly the hippest place on the floor. It was from there that we decided what demonstrations to attend, what concerts to make the trek to, and what to do with our lives."

At the end of their freshman year, Dick had agreed to room again in the fall with Bill and BJ and one or two other friends of Bill's in a "grimy apartment deep within the bowels of Ithaca's College Town," according to Michael. But the apartment needed renovations and they went without heat for most of the fall, along with a crew of workers who started to jackhammer the concrete floor at 7 in the morning, disrupting Dick's carefully crafted study schedule.

Then Bill became the first dropout of the group. As told by several people, a situation arose between Bill and his father who had apparently discovered that BJ was living with Bill. According to sources, Mr. Johnson gave Bill an ultimatum: Cornell or BJ. Bill, the romantic, chose his girl over his school, and they both left Cornell.

They later married.

With Bill gone and the apartment (and his study habits) in complete disarray, Dick moved in with Michael and his roommate, Danny, when Michael added a bed to his second floor room at 505 Wyckoff Avenue in the Cayuga Heights section of Ithaca. "Our bucolic neighborhood was composed of frat houses, family and faculty homes, and many student dwellings," recalled Michael, offering Dick a much-needed more tranquil setting.

"The room rent was a whopping $70, which Dick and I split at $35 apiece," Michael recalled. "Our roommate Danny walked through our room to get to his, but no matter. We soon settled into a routine, cooking together, having dinner at 6, them making the communal trudge over the glorious (but suicide-attracting) suspension bridge which spanned one of Cornell's infamous gorges connecting Cayuga Heights with the Cornell campus mainland.

"Some nights, to save time and trouble, we would splurge and eat at the 'Cosmo' diner in College Town, where $3.00 would buy a full and satisfying meal, in 30 minutes or less. A big night out meant that six to eight of us would migrate, like starved animals, to Howard Johnson for its Wednesday night 'all you can eat' fish fry, for $2.99. The only way we could get to Howard Johnson was by car – Dick's car, to be exact … which cemented his popularity. And better yet, it was an eminently serviceable, fairly ancient, Peugeot 404, a classy vehicle. Light blue and only slightly rusted, the car held 5 or 6 (or 8 or 9, if need be) and soon became our 'go-to' vehicle for all types of excursions up (and down) Lake Cayuga and Ithaca's environs – our ticket to the outside world."

At the beginning of their junior year, Michael met Dick in Flemington and Dick drove the two of them back up to Ithaca.

Dick decided that he wanted to bring his bicycle as a faster means of getting to some of his classes on the Cornell campus.

"We lashed his bike to the back of the car, and proceeded north on Route 81, soon becoming lost in conversation and the radio's blare. Several times during the trip, we both smelled something burning, and pulled over to check the car, opening the hood as if we knew what to do, but finding no obvious fires, continued onward. It was only when we rolled up to 505 Wyckoff Avenue and went to unpack our stuff from the trunk that we realized why the burning smell had stayed with us all the way to Ithaca. Dick's bicycle tire was in the direct path of the Peugeot's exhaust, and was melted straight through. While the beauty of that car was its 'low-slung' appearance, it was apparently less than ideal for hauling bicycles."

It was Dick's car that enabled the activists among them to make road trips: to Boston for the "Beantown" hockey tournament, and to Washington, D.C., for an anti-war demonstration on the Mall.

"In Ithaca," Michael continued, "we would, if feeling financially secure, journey together to the Stagecoach Inn for the one Old Grand Dad bourbon on the rocks that we could afford. Sporting events at Cornell were a bit of an after-thought, but we were lucky enough to experience together, in our freshman year, the glory days of Ed Marinaro, the country's leading tailback, and the exciting Cornell hockey team, then a national power, taking on B.U., B.C., R.P.I., Clarkson, and Saint Lawrence, for national supremacy."

During their junior year, President Nixon imposed wage/price controls to slow the national rate of inflation. At the same time, the boys' landlord imposed a rate increase on their two-bedroom apartment from $135 to $200 a month. The landlord's last name was Banfield, and when there were moments of no heat or hot water, Dick would refer to him as "Banbrains." Michael and Dick felt that the rate increase Banfield imposed was illegal, so they appealed the increase to the Price and Wage Control Board in Buffalo, New York, and won. Thus was the seed planted for Michael to switch majors from pre-med to pre-law. After their legal victory, Dick said to Michael, "You really beat his Banbrains in!"

Their two-bedroom apartment had a mirror-image two-bedroom

apartment on the same floor, separated by a wall. When that other apartment became occupied by Dick and Michael's closest friends, the four decided to take out the wall and make it one big four-bedroom apartment. ("Yes, it's true, Banbrains, we knocked the wall down between the apartments so that we could move readily back and forth. It was all about flow.") This made their now-sprawling second floor apartment an ideal party space, and in November, 1972, they decided it was the perfect place to hold a "blowout Election Eve party."

As Michael explained it, "Dick and I truly believed (which shows you the height of both our delusion and seclusion) that George McGovern (from South Dakota of all places) stood a good chance at defeating the evil, tricky Dick Nixon. Dick Barad (the good Dick) was, as much as anyone, outraged by the atrocities and insanity of the Vietnam War. We both just assumed the rest of the country would also see the light. Ah, for the unreality of youth. As the returns came in, and it became apparent through the early evening (7 p.m.?) that McGovern would win just one state (Massachusetts) in 50, our despair reached new lows. Dick and I (and our merry band) proceeded to drink, and drink, and drink until the night grew long, and morning almost broke. We felt no better in the morning, indeed far worse, but at least we felt that we had suitably commemorated a dark day in American history."

Dick was no different than many of his Cornell counterparts and spent a great deal of time in two local student-run coffee houses: Temple of Zeus in the Arts & Sciences quad, or the Green Dragon in the School of Architecture. "Although we did not know it, these were both precursors in spirit and substance to Starbucks – where you would go to do work, socialize, listen to music, and occasionally have a cup of coffee. Most of all, it was a place for us to debate political issues, to rationalize our non-membership in radical student groups such as SDS, and to chill," Michael explained.

Senior year (1973-74) was, according to Michael, "marked by widespread communal living with the opposite sex - all except Dick, who was still saving himself. We lived, relatively harmoniously, in a 7-bedroom 19th century colonial at the foot of Hudson Street in downtown Ithaca. Dick's Peugeot was key for getting us (way up hill) to class in the morning; if he left before us, it meant hitch-hiking up the hill, which was de rigueur in those days -- a forerunner, perhaps, of HOV lanes. It was at Hudson Street that Dick and I perfected our cooking skills (Army style) for the masses and presiding with others over daily dinners cooked from scratch -- the old standbys of lasagna, chili, and spaghetti."

Chapter 12

Jackie after 1970
The Long-Distance Relationship

When Jackie returned to England in the summer of 1970, she got accepted into an art school, which led her to a degree in Fashion and Design and, ultimately, to a successful career. Dick went to Cornell that fall. The relationship continued, albeit long distance.

The most common and economical way for them to stay connected was to write "long letters" across the Atlantic. There were only a few telephone calls ("the cost was so high"), and visits were restricted to the Christmas or summer holidays. Both Dick and Jackie would make the trans-Atlantic trip when they could. "It was inevitably difficult but in some ways it was good for us both as we were able to concentrate on our work," Jackie said. "I loved to visit Dick and was interested in the life he led at Cornell. When I went up there the life on campus was new to me: the buildings, what people talked about, the way they behaved and dressed, the music, the sweltering summer heat, stories of the deep winter snow. Some things were familiar: the slum landlords, student parties with loud music and bad wine, junk food, the perennial balancing act between a big workload and a social life, (and) the desire to succeed."

Jackie recalled flying to Virginia one summer to visit the Motz family, who had moved to the Lynchburg area in 1971. "It was so nice to see them and I stayed for a few days but coming back to Flemington, I remember walking into the Barad house to a completely rapturous greeting from Dick who ran through the house shouting, "Jackie's back! Jackie's back!" Part of Dick's great charm was his ability to switch from 'serious young man' to crazy and lighthearted in a blink. It was endearing."

In the summer of 1971, Jackie and Dick decided that they would like to take a trip through Europe. They would spend many nights camping under the stars.

They borrowed Jackie's mother's yellow Triumph Herald that they referred to as the "Yellow Peril" and took the ferry from

England to France. They drove through France with only a few minor setbacks, like locking the keys inside the car and almost getting arrested by the police for attempting to break into their own car.

Halfway across Italy, The Peril started making "appalling noises" as they drove at 70 mph down the Autostrada. They discovered that if we went faster it didn't sound so bad. But they were eventually forced to pull into a service station to get help.

Jackie remembered, "This resulted in my getting out of the car to let the engineer climb in, which resulted in Dick driving off down the motorway WITHOUT ME, which resulted in me being left alone at a service station somewhere in Italy, with no ID, no money, no telephone, and wearing only a tee shirt and a pair of shorts! Not an ideal situation."

Dick thought he was just being directed to the service area, but the service area was on the other side of the highway which resulted in "poor Dick finding himself, to his horror, driving back into the motorway traffic accompanied by an engineer who didn't speak English, having left his girlfriend behind," Jackie recalled.

"Hours later I spotted Dick again, frantically waving to me from the other side of six lanes of fast moving traffic after he had left the motorway, paid the toll, rejoined the motorway and finally retraced his route to end up on the 'service' side. I was extremely relieved to see him."

The problem with the car was a tear on the inside of a tire, banging against the wheel arch. They had been incredibly lucky that it hadn't burst as they were driving.

They drove on to Yugoslavia where they lost all their important documents on the first evening. One of them had placed the wallet containing their money, passports, return ferry tickets, and all other travel documents on the roof of the car after filling the car with gas, and then drove off with the wallet still on the roof. They didn't realize what had happened until it was too late and too far away to try to go back.

As Jackie remembered, "Trying to travel in a Communist country without ID or travel documents isn't a good plan. We ended up the next morning face to face with a very large policewoman straight from Central Casting who sat underneath a photograph of General Tito and did not look happy. In the end, we got off lightly and were sent across country to Zagreb where there was both an American and British embassy to get replacement ID. Zagreb was a friendly place and Dick and I both really liked the Yugoslavian people. It was appalling to think of what happened to that country only a few years later."

Using their new IDs, they drove back across Europe with two sheets of paper written in Serbo-Croatian which no one could understand but did have their photographs attached, and amazingly they were allowed to cross the borders. Thanks to Dick's American Express card which he somehow still had, they had enough cash to survive.

Jackie continued the story. "We made our way back across southern Europe, it was chaotic and fun, and by the time we made it to the south of France the old car was just about still going, although by then the silencer had dropped off so the noise we made when going through towns and villages was quite impressive. Also, by now the car didn't really take to climbing mountains very well so that we had to stop every fifteen minutes to take off the radiator cap to release the steam to let her cool down. It took us ages to get over the Pyrenees.

"Getting back across the English Channel was complicated by an international money crisis which made releasing money to pay for new ferry tickets a near thing. I hadn't been in contact with my family since Yugoslavia as I didn't want them to worry about the lack of documents. What Dick and I didn't know was that our papers had all been sent back to my home by an Austrian tourist who had found them on the floor of the Yugoslavian petrol station. Naturally, my mother got hold of these and couldn't imagine how we could manage without them...visions of Dick and I in a Yugoslavian goal (jail)!

"So, along with dozens of other cars, Dick and I drove off the ferry and, randomly, up to one of several immigration booths to present our documents. In our case this meant two scruffy pieces of paper written in Serbo-Croatian with our photos on. A surprising thing happened. The immigration officer examined our papers, looked at us carefully, then broke into a large smile and said, 'Oh, you're Dick and Jackie! I spoke to your mother this morning. She has phoned every port on the South coast of England begging us to let you in. Apparently, she has your passports!' It was nothing short of humbling really."

Eventually, though, the gaps between letters grew longer and longer. Education and the respective career paths each had chosen took its toll, especially on Jackie. "Dick was focused on medicine," Jackie remembered. "It was important, and in comparison, I felt pretty lightweight despite all the work I was putting in. I am so grateful for the time we did have together which was so special. I have always been so grateful for those extraordinary years with Dick."

Michael Zweig graduated from Cornell a semester earlier than Dick and missed, in his words, "Dick's period of agonizing as to which medical school (unbelievably competitive at the time) would accept him." Knowing that Dick's father was a doctor, and that older brother David was also about to take the plunge in medicine, "Dick undoubtedly felt no small amount of pressure to succeed. We told him that if he did not deserve admission to med school, no one did. He did get in finally, and in typical Dick fashion, worked extremely hard, so much so that I barely saw him during our first year of graduate school."

By that time, Michael had given up on a career in medicine, and had entered law school, presumably inspired by his legal victory over Banbrains.

In 1974, Dick graduated from Cornell and he was very focused on getting into medical school right away. It was about this time that Dick and Jackie broke up. The strain of an international long-distance relationship between two people who were headed down very separate life paths took its toll. It had run its course. There remained strong feelings on both of their parts and it wasn't without pain when it ended.

Chapter 13

Dr. Dick and Dr. Nancy
The woman who became Dick's wife

David Barad had graduated from college in 1972 and had applied at the time to medical school but did not get accepted. David decided to go to Boston to graduate school and his then-girlfriend Iris, now his wife, went with him. David took grad school courses for two years and, in 1974, both he and Dick applied to get into NJ School of Medicine and Dentistry, Rutgers University.

David believes to this day that Dick got accepted on merit but that he, David, had help from his father getting in. Regardless, they both entered medical school in the fall of 1974 and quickly became known as "the brothers" in their class.

Nancy Scattergood entered Dick's life in September, 1974. They met on the first day of classes at the College of Medicine and Dentistry. Dick and Nancy were both studying to be doctors.

According to Nancy, "I do remember meeting Dick, milling around in the central hall, I think at a break, knowing no one, in a new place, being excited. I met Dick and David together, memorable because they were 'the brothers' in the class. I also met David's new wife Iris, who had taken a job as secretary to the Dean of the medical school. By late October, Dick and I were "a thing," though each of us still had old 'significant others' that were slightly in the picture."

"My college relationship, Bill, wasn't destined to last a long-term separation. He was attending medical school in Virginia. We had hoped to get into the same school, but that didn't happen. We did do the six-hour drive a couple of times that first semester. He thought that I should give up my aspirations to become a doctor and follow him. I didn't. He also felt I should eventually drive a station wagon, while he would drive a fancy car. We would live in the suburbs. Ultimately, our vision of life didn't match when looked at critically."

Nancy was a product of her era. This was 1974, when women were finding empowerment where there had been little to none before. "Women felt we could do anything and set out to do it," Nancy explained. "Medical school classes, at this time, were about 10% women. The world was there for the taking and I was ready to take it.

"Dick was there (if you can't be with the one you love, love the one you're with), and I was ready to try new things. New York City was a mystery to me as I grew up on a South Jersey truck farm." For their first date, Dick asked her to go to see The Laser Show at the Hayden Planetarium in New York City. "I had no interest in NYC," Nancy said, "but I was game and it was fun. The evening went well and from then on we found reason to be together."

On either their first or second date, a ritual was established. "I vaguely remember having to go the Barad's house for dinner because Dot was home. Dot being home became a joke with us, as we had to go to the Barad home whenever she was home to see her. It was not a bad joke, but one that gave us a laugh."

Soon they were spending more and more time together. "We would study for about eight hours a day. Studying was interesting. Neither of our apartments was conducive to studying, so we would find alcoves in the medical school and spread out. Dick could concentrate on studies/goals better than anyone I knew. It was good for me to be with someone who actually could study for hours at a time. Being with him made studying much more interesting."

They would also meet at the local pub for a Friday beer, or go to the Barad's .... because Dot was home. "We were only 22, after all. I would need to have a diversion now and then, and for that I think I was useful to him," she added.

"By Thanksgiving, although our other Significant Others occasionally entered our lives, we were a couple - and certainly a couple within our new life of Medical School. Throughout our time together, we laughed a lot."

During their second year of medical school, Dick and Nancy each had a separate room in a 5-person house. The third year, they shared a 2-bedroom apartment with another couple, and during their last year of med school (1977-78), they had an apartment of their own.

In the fourth year of medical school, students must decide

where they want to spend the next four years of residency. They apply to teaching medical centers early in their last academic year, arrange for interviews, and then create a "wish list" of places where they would like to serve in order of preference. Those wish lists are entered into a computer and one day in March, every fourth-year med student in the country finds out where he or she is assigned to residency.

While Dick and Nancy were talking about where they wanted to go, it became increasingly clear that they wanted to stay together. So, an added layer of concern to the residency application process was that they had to find someplace that would accept both of them. Dick made this stipulation very clear in his personal statement that was attached to each application. "My most important personal involvement has been with my fiancée, Nancy Scattergood…. The most important factor in both our lives is for us to stay together and we expect to be married prior to the beginning of our residencies…. Under the rules provided by the NIRMP (National Resident Matching Program) for married and engaged couples, we will be attempting to gain acceptance to a residency program prior to the match next March. If for some reason you feel that you would be unable to accept a couple under any circumstances, we hope that you would inform us of this fact prior to our interview."

This personal statement went out with each application, and is typical of Dick on several levels: 1) he made his position abundantly clear, 2) he seemed to throw down a challenge - "both of us or neither of us;" and 3) he had done his research and knew his rights, and wasn't afraid to let anyone know that he knew. (*See Dick's complete Personal Statement, Appendix G*).

The decision to get married was made jointly during their last year of med school around December, 1977. "There was no romantic proposal (again this was the 1970s and we were a bit hippyish)," Nancy said, "and no ring." They had been discussing the topic of marriage for a while.

"As was usual with Dick, he only would do things when he was ready and felt it was right. Most of the time that was great, but when coordinating with someone else it can trip one up at times. I was ready to get married earlier than he was and in fact had started looking around to see if there might be other possibilities. I don't know if he felt this separating or he just became 'ready,' but we then told our parents and started planning a wedding."

They also narrowed down their preferences for residency. According to Nancy, "Our first choice was Rochester, New York; second choice was Madison, Wisconsin; third, Lancaster, Pennsylvania; and fourth was Charleston, South Carolina. I can't really recall any of the whys, though I do remember Dick saying that he wasn't sure that he could take a place seriously that had palm trees in the parking lot. We were shocked that we ended up in Wisconsin as that program had a strong preference for training Wisconsin residents that would more likely practice in Wisconsin."

The last two-month rotation in medical school, during March and April, 1978, was an elective. Nancy chose to do some Third World medicine in Haiti at a Baptist mission hospital while Dick went to San Francisco. Mail arrived only twice a week in Haiti. There were no telephones and, though she loved it there, Nancy was lonely.

"While there, we learned that we were 'placed' at the University of Wisconsin in Madison for our Family Practice residency," Nancy said. They were matched by a computer. "I had to take a tap-tap (local truck transport) into Cap Haitian," Nancy said. "Two hours on bumpy roads to call through those old long distance relays to find this all out. But it was good to talk with Dick, the real reason to call."

Dick and Nancy were married on Memorial Day, May 29, 1978, three weeks after graduation from medical school. About 200 people showed up at Nancy's parents' house in Bordentown, New Jersey, including many friends from medical school. The wedding was held on the lawn and the reception was in a large tent. Nancy's father mowed a corner of the front wheat field to accommodate the tent. The Rabbi had to hurry the ceremony because he could see rain clouds coming, and afterwards there was a double rainbow, which Dot later described as "the most beautiful she had ever seen." Bill Johnson and his band played, and band members included Jim Gilheany, Carol Brooks, Juli Davidson and Robbie Blumenthal."

"The only bad taste of the day," Nancy said, "was we think 'the band' left with all the extra food, booze and even the wedding cake. We hadn't eaten much and were planning to enjoy an evening meal of leftovers with our families."

The Zweigs and the Barads attended each other's weddings, as Dick knew Michael's wife (Michelle) from their days at Cornell. "Michelle remembers his kindness when, following an off-campus celebration where we had too much to drink, he held her hair back as she leaned to the side of the road and puked her guts out. That image – reflecting Dick's gentleness, his thoughtfulness, and valor - still endures."

Dick and Nancy's wedding was also memorable. "No catering hall for them," Michael remembered. "Instead, the park-like surroundings of Nancy's family's southern New Jersey farm. And I mean farm – acres and acres of cornfields, and hay, and manure. And a glorious wedding; that is, until the darkest of storm clouds emerged, almost tornado-like, to puncture the stillness and calm of that scene."

July 1st is the turnover time in medicine, where new interns/residents start and everyone moves up in position by one notch. "Try not to get sick in early July," Nancy warned, "at least not at a teaching center." They were due to report to Madison, Wisconsin, on July 1, 1978, so in June they spent 10 days on "a really glorious honeymoon trip" to Greece.

"The residency years" of 1978-1982 found Dick and Nancy "a little shocked" to find themselves in Wisconsin. "Residency: finally making money," Nancy recalled, "working long hours (except when on an easy rotation). ICU call, delivering babies, pediatrics, hospital rounds, clinic work, learning to manage chronic illness, learning to act like a doctor. Dick was able to do that last one easily, whether it was his nature, or because he had his father as a model. And of course, Dick, being Dick, was chief resident our last year (from July, 1980-June, 1981)."

When they moved there, they bought cross-country skis, although neither of them had ever done cross-country skiing before. They also bought a tent and camped in Door County (the trendy pinkie finger that pokes into Lake Michigan), and once canoed down the Wisconsin River.

"One November-December we did an obstetrics rotation in Green Bay," Nancy remembered. "We delivered many babies, we were the first residents ever in that hospital, we did 24 hours on/ 24 hours off, and we saw each other at breakfast to sign out. Another two-month rotation was on 'rural rotation' where each resident worked in a small Wisconsin town. We were two towns apart and saw each other on weekends. In our spare time, we took a moonlighting job in a small ER south of Madison. We had a lot of energy in those days."

Brian Lochen, M.D., recalls a time when he shared a pediatrics rotation with Dick. On the day Brian's daughter Sara was born, he was scheduled to do the rotation first, so he asked Dick to switch shifts with him, and Dick agreed.

A young boy, about two years old, named Brian Braun was admitted during the time Dick was on duty. No one on the medical staff could figure out what was wrong with Brian, so Dick ordered a spinal tap to be performed, and Brian was diagnosed with meningitis. He was treated accordingly and Dick took special interest in watching out for the boy during his recovery. The boys' parents had nicknamed him "Boober." Dick gently suggested to the parents that "Boober" might not be such a great nickname for a boy who was on a ventilator and who already had a clubfoot.

Years later, Brian Lochen recalled that he became aware of a "Boomer" Braun who was a star soccer player at local Madison West High School, a year or two ahead of his daughter Sara. Brian also recalled reading a story about "Boomer" Braun and about how he overcame a serious illness and a clubfoot as a child. Brian is convinced that this is the same boy whose life was saved by Dick.

Nancy remembered "a random thought" about Dick:

"Our strong points are often also our weak ones. Dick was wonderful at carefully, methodically thinking through a problem and forming a solution. As a medical partner this was invaluable to me and I still feel 'not quite whole' in my medical practice. I'm a 'gut jumper' (actually a reasonable way to come to a medical conclusion) but one needs to then backtrack and figure out why that intuitive feeling is real or not. In this we worked as a team. I could formulate a theory and he could process it logically.

"It was also invaluable to have a bed partner who was also a medical partner, a quick consult when sleep was preferable to making quick and good medical decisions. (Also, he was a very deep sleeper, and when sleep-deprived could give orders in his sleep, I learned to listen and intervene when I knew he was asleep.)

"So.... that being a strength, for a life partner, it could be frustrating and prevent spontaneity, though I believe this actually rarely happened. A random and spontaneous garden that might not be perfect in August wasn't an acceptable alternative for him. Though I have to admit, his need to think things through may have kept me out of some trouble even if at times I just wanted to get on with it."

Chapter 14

Africa and Bennington (1982)
Dreams realized

Africa... a dream that Dick and Nancy shared.

Nancy remembers: "We were without obligations: no kids, no possessions, and we were finishing residency. My work in Haiti had been very enticing and we both wanted to see a bit more of the world. We were both drawn to Africa. I can't really explain that, though both of us liked to travel and we had a bit of the back-pack travel left in us.

"We looked around for sponsors. The Peace Corps wanted a two-year commitment and we would be caring for other Peace Corps volunteers, not Africans. Concern, a wonderful Catholic group that sponsors volunteers mostly to Central and South America, had a six-month spot in a remote village in Sierra Leone, Serabu. This seemed perfect. We would practice medicine, have an experience, then return (we both turned 30 in Africa) ready to take on life as family doctors in the U.S. We actually stayed for almost a year, but three months of this was traveling around Africa, Israel, and England. We had to return by August 7th for Dot's wedding. There are years in one's life that are extraordinary, this was one of them."

They returned to the U.S. and turned their attention to finding a town and start a practice. According to Nancy: "We looked around, mostly in the northeast and though there were several possible places to settle, we both felt we wanted to be in Bennington, Vermont, the minute we drove into town. (Plus, we liked the green license plate.)

"We had decided that we wanted to practice in the same group, sharing a joint practice, call it what you want. We wanted partners as we needed some time away from work together as well. Sandy Bidner, M.D. decided to retire. (He had a solo practice in Bennington for five years.) He had persuaded a young family practitioner (also known as an "FP") Edd Lyon, M.D. who was in a group north of town to join him prior to his leaving. With Edd's patients following him and Sandy's full practice, they needed another doctor to be there when Sandy left. We met a Bennington FP, Bruce Nash, M.D., while at a Family Practice Conference in San Francisco. Bruce was recruiting for his practice, but didn't want two doctors. He directed us to Sandy and Edd.

"We were unconcerned that there was a practice ready for only one doctor. We felt (and rightly so, I might add) that we could build our practice without much trouble. We both wanted to live in the country, and in Bennington we could be three miles from the hospital and be surrounded by 100 acres, looking at a national forest and the ridge that holds the Appalachian Trail."

They moved to Bennington in November, 1982, and rented a house on South Stream Road that they eventually bought. They started to work in their family practice on January 2, 1983. Sandy Bidner M.D. left six months later. "We did the full range of family practice," said Nancy, "including delivering babies. It was another high time, like Africa.

"We were also ready to start a family," Nancy added, "though this for us wasn't quite as easy as most. Infertility is a major life nuisance, though it was my issue, not Dick's."

The first weekend of May each year is the 10K Bennington Road Race. Dick was a 'jogger' for health and fun, but he decided he wanted to run in the 1983 race, so he extended his "jogging" to actual run training. On race day, he wore his worn-out grey Cornell tee shirt and was beaten by Jessie Donavan, his six-year-old neighbor who was running in her first race with her father Pete, a retired marathon runner who also beat Dick. This became one of Dick's favorite stories because he thought it was highly amusing to be beaten by a six-year-old. (In 1987, Pete wore the now-holey grey Cornell tee shirt when he ran in the Bennington Road Race.)

Chapter 15

1983
The First Illness

Dick first got sick in September, 1983. On Rosh Hashanah, September 8, the Barad family members were all supposed to meet at the Jewish Community Center in Flemington, NJ, for services. Dick and Nancy were late and the rest of the family wondered where they were.

It turned out that Dick had developed a terrible headache that morning. Then he began throwing up and it was not relieved by the usual means. Rather than to try to make the four-hour trip to New Jersey, Nancy instead had him taken to the hospital in Bennington. For perhaps a month, Dick had been having some minor headaches that he thought were TMJ related - temporomandibular joint disorder, or TMJ syndrome. This is an umbrella term covering inflammation of the temporomandibular joint, which connects the jawbone to the skull.

"We were in our first year of practice, in a new house, in a new town and stress is just part of that," Nancy remembered. "He also occasionally 'stepped out of line', in that he stepped into my line and made me either move over or trip. He did have the ability to have tunnel vision about what he was doing or thinking, and I attributed this to inattention.

"I was on call that day, and our receptionist, Rita McPhee, was also having a headache and was vomiting. We thought that these were a virus, perhaps a viral meningitis. I asked the neurologist on call, Tom Snyder, M.D., to meet us all in the ER (in Bennington) to help sort it all out as I was too close to both situations.

X-rays showed that there was "a big thing in his head that shouldn't be there." Dr. Snyder, the neurologist, showed Nancy the x-rays and they took them in to Dick. The idea of Dick getting a CT scan was floated, but this was in the early stage of CT scans and the hospital in Bennington didn't have a CT machine. The closest one at the time happened to be in Troy, New York, more than 30 miles away, so instead, Dr. Snyder performed a spinal tap on both Dick and Rita.

"Rita had typical spinal fluid for a viral meningitis," Nancy remembered, "and though this is a nuisance, recovery happens in the course of time. Dick, however, did not have the typical spinal fluid; he had a large amount of protein in the fluid."

Dr. Snyder asked another internist to see Dick for a second opinion, and together they felt Dick needed to have a head CT to see if there was a tumor. They contacted the authorities in Troy and scheduled a CT scan for the next morning.

During the night, around midnight, another neurologist was now on call. He stopped by to see Dick and did a second spinal tap, which should not have been done so soon after the first one. Nancy was not at the hospital at the time and she believes that Dick may have even given permission for, or even wanted, the second spinal tap to be done but didn't want to bother her or consult with her because he didn't want to make a fuss.

The danger in performing the second spinal tap when there is a tumor present is that when the fluid is removed from the spinal column below, the tips of the brain will herniate into the hole in the skull that the spinal column and midbrain pass through (the foramen magnum). This usually results in death, but Dick had a very large foramen magnum and didn't die with the second spinal tap but got a massive headache that morphine wouldn't help.

This second neurologist wouldn't respond when Dick complained of his terrible headache so the nurses called Nancy. "I came in, called Tom (Snyder), and he started high doses of steroids that relieved the headache."

Shortly after, they set out for Troy and had the CT performed, which confirmed a large cerebellar tumor. The cerebellum is in the back, lower part of the brain and is the center for coordination and sight.

It was decided that Dick needed to go to Massachusetts General Hospital in Boston. David was based in Boston at the time and may have helped get Dick a referral there.

"I believe, when we actually had something solid to react to, we went into clinical mode," Nancy recalled later. "It is very useful to be able to intellectualize these things and we were well-trained in how to do it. I suspect his brother David and father Gerald did the same thing. We had a finding and this is what you do.

"We were referred to Mass General, where a 'world famous

posterior fossa' neurosurgeon resided, Dr. Oegerman. The actual diagnosis of the astrocytoma and how aggressive it was had to wait until the surgery, which happened soon, I believe on September 24 or so. Dr. Oegerman resected (surgically removed) the tumor microscopically. The operation took eight hours."

During the surgery, a piece of the tumor was sent to the lab to get a 'wet reading' to give the surgeon a better idea of what he/she is dealing with. This is not the final diagnosis, but it is usually pretty reliable.

Nancy remembered, "Our friend from medical school, Ray Maciewicz, was practicing neurology at Mass General and was the 'admitting' physician. He came to us (David, Bea and Jerry, and me) where we were waiting, gave us the 'wet reading/frozen section' diagnosis." He confirmed her worst fears, a Grade 4 (the worst) Astrocytoma, also known as glioblastoma." This particular type of brain cancer is typically found in younger children, not older adults.

"I had been wistfully hoping for a funny abscess caused by some African parasite, but that was not to be."

"I left the hospital and just walked, Ray followed and walked with me. By the time we returned, the operation was over, we met with the surgeon, I don't remember much of what he said, but he confirmed the diagnosis."

When Dick woke up in the ICU and was told the diagnosis, all he said was, "Isn't that a tumor that kids get?" Nancy marveled at how he remembered that. "That was just one of those pieces of information that is crammed into our heads in medical school, rarely to ever be needed."

According to Nancy, recovery from brain surgery is actually easier than from bowel surgery since there are no eating issues. "As long as there are no seizures and one's balance is ok, it's quick and Dick did quite well. I think that we were home within a week."

When Dick was discharged, his neighbor, Peter Donavan, who along with his daughter had beaten Dick in the 10K Bennington Road Race earlier that year, had a Suburban that would accommodate a mattress in the back, so he volunteered to drive Dick home. Dick lay on the mattress on the trip home and along the way, he expressed a desire for a hot dog. Both Nancy and Peter were afraid Dick would choke on it, but Dick wanted a hot dog so they got him a hot dog. He survived the swallowing of it.

The prognosis was not good. The primary objective of the surgery was to remove as many tumorous cells as possible. But Grade 4 is the worst level, with a low survival rate – less than 3% will last for three years or more. The tumors were known to be able to spread quickly and grow very fast, even after surgery. The doctors gave Dick only a 50% chance of surviving a year.

From that point, Dick and Nancy focused on making treatment decisions, hoping that the tumor was gone. "We decided to do local radiation to the posterior fossa part of the brain, rather than total brain and spinal cord radiation," she recalled, "as total radiation likely would decrease one's ability to reason, and that was an unacceptable outcome. Turns out, it may have been a fatal decision, or maybe not, who knows?"

When the tumor returned, it was in his spinal cord.

After the surgery wound healed, Dick headed to Boston every Monday and returned home to Bennington every Friday for a six-week course of radiation. He couldn't drive, so friends showed up from all over to drive him. Peter Donavan, his neighbor, took him down once, Nancy drove him, or he took the bus. While in Boston, he stayed with brother David and Iris and their young daughter Alexis.

Dick's first day back at work was on Christmas Day, 1983, just short of a year after they had begun their practice. "We let him take calls and he was happy to," according to Nancy. But they also had to face the very uncertain future. "We sat down to go over how we would change our lives," Nancy recalled, "knowing that he had a 50% chance of a years' survival, or as we saw it, a 50 % chance of cure. It was one or the other."

They realized that they didn't want to change very much. They were living in Vermont where they wanted to live. They had their own family medical practice, doing what they wanted to do. So, the major things in life – where you are living and what you are doing – they were happy with.

What changes they did feel were important were things they could add to their lives. They both wanted to start a family. And Dick especially wanted to get a dog. He was a big fan of a song made famous by the band The Byrds in the late 1960s called *Old*

Blue. It was a favorite song of Dick's, as well as the rest of the Barad family.

Within a very short period of time, Dick and Nancy adopted a black Newfoundland dog that they named Blue.

"It was nice knowing that we were exactly where we wanted to be in life," Nancy said.

Chapter 16

1984-1985
Living with hope, and the arrival of Leah

Dick and Nancy had planned a trip to Cancun, Mexico, the week after Christmas, 1983, and despite Dick just having come off radiation therapy, they made the trip. Either on that trip or shortly thereafter, Nancy finally became pregnant. They had been trying for a while and both were thrilled with the news.

Their daughter was born on October 8, 1984. She was a breech baby so a Caesarian section was performed. According to her mother, she was a "perfect" baby, and she was named Leah.

"Leah's name is two-fold," Nancy said. "My middle name is Lee and I'd always wanted to actually be called Lee, though never pulled it off. Leah also works as a Hebrew name, so there didn't have to be two names." Apparently unbeknownst to them at the time, Leah was also the name of one of Dick's great-great grandmothers from Russia.

Nancy continued, "I remained a Quaker and wasn't completely comfortable with all of the Jewish traditions, though I did find that most are rooted in good sense and human needs. Her birth is, of course, one of the high points of my life, and I think Dick's.

"And so... we lived life as we had set up. We continued to practice medicine with Edd Lyon as a third partner, added a fourth, Barbara Raskin; planned a family; got a dog; kept our cat, Brima; all the while knowing that this 50 % hung over our heads. But... since we were where we wanted to be, we kept at it and had a very fulfilling year in 1984."

Early in 1985, with the hope that he was cured, Dick started 'training' to once again run in the Bennington Road Race in May. But he was unable to run, and he developed headaches. Dick and Nancy both knew the tumor was back, so he soon returned to Boston for radiation treatment.

In the throes of all they had to go through in the next few months, Dick had the presence of mind to do two things that would have a tremendous impact on Leah in later years. He wanted to pick out a ring that Nancy would give Leah on her sixteenth birthday. So, he had Nancy go to local jewelers and explain the situation, and they, unbelievably, would give her different opals that she would take back to the house until Dick selected just the right one. Then Nancy had that opal turned into a ring, and she kept it locked up and gave it to Leah when she turned 16.

Leah rarely took the ring off after that. In fact, she was so moved that she wrote a sonnet about it:

The Opal

A golden ring around my finger lies,
Pale-bright colors swirl, an eye to the past.
A treasure given as a father dies,
Along with the questions I've always asked.

The circuit continues, coiled and curled
Around my finger and mind it does spin,
The more you reflect the further you're twirled,
The end is the same as where you begin.

All I envision is that golden prize.
Memories never experienced flash,
But none can I witness with my own eyes,
Though they stay with me 'til the very last.

The ring is clouded by the constant sound
Of memories always, but never quite round.

Unfortunately, the ring was lost years later. Leah is not sure, but she believes she was in the lawn of their home in the winter throwing snowballs. That night, she realized the ring was missing. They could not find it in the snow, nor could they find it in the spring when the snow melted. Leah believes that it was lost in a part of the yard that gets cut for hay, and that sometime over the years it got caught up in the hay baling. They never did find it. It was in that same part of the yard that would later serve as the setting for her wedding,

The other thing Dick did that had a profound effect on his daughter years later was, shortly before his death, he dictated to Nancy his final message to Leah that was included in her first birthday card. Dick's message was simple and poignant: Be wise, know yourself, and have a good life. I did, it was just too short.

Nancy brought Dick home from Boston at the end of July with the expectation that Dick only had about two more weeks to live. "He was, at times, coherent enough to grasp this," Nancy recalled. "During one of his lucid times, I asked him what it was like to know he had only two weeks to live, and he replied that it 'felt symmetrical,' but couldn't really define that further. He lived about two more months. He was part of the decision to not pursue another opinion and to let the tumor take its course, though in less lucid times he would wonder why we weren't doing more."

It was about this time that Dick spoke with Jackie for the last time. As Dot recalled: "Nancy and I decided we should place the phone call since Jackie was important… if not just to Dick but to our whole family and it felt right to give him a chance to say goodbye.

"So, we placed the call and Nancy and I left Dick on the phone with Jackie so we bowed out of the room. We both thought he could use the privacy to say whatever he wanted. We both were busy with our babies. Noah and Leah always enjoyed each other even when they were this young and they were a break from the heartbreak of illness.

"We left Dick on the phone with Jackie and after 10 minutes or so we went back in the room. Dick was holding the phone, but he had had a small seizure and was just frozen holding the phone. We had no idea how long he had been like that but I kept thinking, 'Oh my, we have horrified poor Jackie by first calling out of the blue with no warning shots and now she would have no idea what was happening with silence on the other end of the phone.' I took the phone from him and, yes, Jackie was still on the line. We said our goodbyes and then Nancy and I both felt so bad/embarrassed and had hoped Dick was able to communicate for some of the call.

"Years later, Jackie told me how meaningful the call was and how much she appreciated the chance to say goodbye. That made me feel so much better."

A few weeks before Dick passed away, the Barad family gathered in Bennington for what would be the final weekend together. "Dick was failing fast and we all needed to come to Vermont to enjoy what we had," Dot recalled. "I remember the weekend to be joyous and sad... great being together yet the oncoming dread."

Present were brother Bob; sister Dot and her husband Bruce Waterman, along with their baby Noah, who was a little more than a year old; brother David and his wife Iris, along with their two children Alexis (5) and Justin. (Justin is two months older than Noah and Noah is four months older than Leah); and Jerry and Bea. Also included was very close childhood friend, Fred Huber and his very pregnant wife Cindy, who was almost full term in her pregnancy. The couple had to fly up from Ashville, North Carolina, to be with the Barad family.

Fred became David's close friend while they were in the Delaware Township School and he was a frequent visitor at the Barad dinner table. David and Fred went off to college at the same time, to different schools, and when Fred came home he would continue to visit the Barad house, even if David wasn't home.

Dot kids him now, saying Dick inherited Fred from David and she inherited Fred from Dick. All three of the older Barad children had many adventures with Fred, including many summer night drives to the movies either in Somerville or Princeton or Flemington.

Dick and Nancy had built a solarium with a hot tub in it in their Bennington home. That night, when the entire family had gathered together, after dinner everyone was getting in and out of the hot tub. At one point, all the guys - David, Bob, Fred, Dick and Jerry - were all in the tub together. The men were singing *Old Blue* and the ladies were laughing and taking photos. Suddenly, Dick and Nancy's dog Blue pushed through the screen window and jumped into the room. "We were all laughing so hard," Dot recalled. "For a moment there, for the very last moment, everything was okay, normal, and happy. It was magic in a way... and then it was over.

"I know Dick does not want to be remembered by his illness, but on the other hand, being with him, though it was difficult as it was, when I look back, I felt lucky to be able to share these moments with him as well," Dot remembered wistfully.

Nancy also remembered, "He did enjoy seeing those family members and friends who were able to visit during those two months. We had a wonderful family party, all getting into the hot tub, and I believe Fred and Cindy were there. He held onto that good feeling and wanted me to keep that going after everyone had left and I couldn't."

Nancy tried to maintain a semblance of normalcy even facing Dick's decline. "Dot and Bruce, David, his college roommates, and Tom Vaughn all stopped by. Pete Donavan helped shave him as did our partner Edd Lyon. Food arrived nightly. After about six weeks I hired a nurse for daytime and went back to work for 3-4 hours a day, I think to bring some sanity back to my life."

When he came home from the hospital, Dick had little use of his legs, and this worsened. The tumor had surrounded his spinal cord, then spread to his midbrain. He slowly lost sight and the ability to think quickly. Sometimes, in a group, he would answer a question from several minutes earlier. He slowly stopped being able to swallow. He became weak and needed full care.

As he neared the end, a bed was brought downstairs and set up in the living room so Dick wouldn't have to negotiate stairs. A shower was installed in the hot tub room. Bruce Waterman, Dot's husband, built ramps so that Nancy could wheel Dick outside to sit in the fall air and have picnics.

Nancy's brother was to be married on the 21st of September in Maryland and Nancy had cancelled her plane tickets, but three of her neighbors - Terry Ehrich, Neil Moss, and Pete Donavan - hired a private plane from a friend of Pete's who ran an air service, so Nancy flew on a six-seater private plane with Leah out of Bennington airport to a small airport near the wedding site in Maryland. The pilot, a friend of Pete's, waited by the plane. Nancy's sister and her husband picked them up and drove them to the wedding, and they were able to stay for the reception, a welcome six-hour break. Dot, Bruce, and Noah came to care for Dick while she was away.

"Dot and I 'joked' that while I was gone, Dick could die," Nancy said, "but it was a chance I wanted to take."

Gradually, Dick was only able to recognize and communicate

with Nancy, his sister Dot, and his brother David.

The night before he died, Dick developed a fever and Nancy was pretty sure he had developed pneumonia. After discussing it with Jerry, David, and Tom Snyder, his doctor in Bennington, who Nancy called "a wonderful neurologist and friend," the decision was made not to treat the pneumonia. "Perhaps with treatment he could have lived another week or so," Nancy recalled.

"I knew he was going to die that evening," Nancy said, "so Sally Donavan (Pete's wife) took Leah for the evening and I sat, reading and waiting. I wanted to be alone with him and it was very peaceful. He just stopped breathing. I first called Sally to get Leah home, then called Tom Snyder to come and pronounce him, then all the family, though I have no clear recollection. All the neighbors moved the bed back upstairs. Leah slept with me and I believe Sally spent the night, though I had no need of company."

On September 24, 1985, David had just returned home from Kol Nidre, the evening service on the beginning of Yom Kippur, when Nancy called to tell him that Dick had died around sundown. Because Yom Kippur is a holy Jewish holiday, it gave Nancy 48 hours to prepare for the funeral rather than the customary 24 hours.

Dick was first sick on Rosh Hashanah 1983 and died on Yom Kippur 1985. The family has always felt it significant that Dick became sick and then died on the two most important days in the Jewish calendar. Rosh Hashanah is the new year when the book of life is opened and God is said to begin evaluation of each Jewish soul. Yom Kippur is known as the Day of Remembrance when names are inscribed for the next year. Thus, by dying on Yom Kippur, Dick received the full measure of the previous year.

It was two weeks before Leah's first birthday.

Chapter 17

The cemetery

The day of the funeral saw Hurricane Gloria bearing down on New England and it almost disrupted the service.

As the cars in the funeral processional passed through the entrance to The Park Lawn Cemetery just outside of Bennington, the passengers were greeted by a sign that announced: "No artificial flowers Apr 1 to Nov 1." Jerry Barad read the sign and said aloud, "That's nice."

To this day, when Dot goes to visit Dick's grave, she places three of something on his headstone, a Jewish tradition according to Dot. Most of the time it's three Oreo cookies.

"Why Oreos?" she asked. "He loved them. When he was in college my Mom used to send him packages of cookies in the mail. When Dick turned 21, his roommates had a big party for him. The day of his birthday, a package arrived from my Mom and everyone in the house thought it was Dick's birthday present. My parents do not give birthday presents … they are just not wired that way. (When my own children were little I would buy presents and put my parents' names on them.) So everyone in the house was excited to see what was in the package. Dick kept saying, 'It's not what you think... really, it won't be anything.' But everyone insisted he open the package during the party. So, after the cake there was the package. Again, Dick tried to tell them it was nothing as he started opening the brown wrapper. The box inside said Nikon Camera on the outside of it. Now everyone was really excited and Dick kept saying, 'There is a mistake here.' When he opened the box, it had a package of Oreo cookies in it. He thought that was great, but his roommates were all disappointed for him and it was a letdown for the party.

"But Dick was happy to have the Oreos. He knew the timing was just coincidental, but they were his favorite cookies, and they made him happy."

Which is why Leah and Dot leave Oreos at his grave when they visit.

A colleague wife watched Leah at home during the funeral.

Afterwards, family and friends gathered at Nancy's house. It was full of people and there was food for all, although Nancy still does not remember how it all got arranged.

Gradually, everyone left except Dot, who spent the night there. She remembers hearing the wind and rain from the hurricane all night and feeling awful that Dick was outside.

Dick was gone, but the ties that bound this family together never broke. Nancy is still considered to be a beloved member of the Barad family and still joins in for family occasions when she can. She and Leah spent that Thanksgiving with the Barads in Flemington.

Dot spent every summer in Bennington visiting Nancy and Leah, and they in turn visited Dot and her sons Noah and Aaron when they lived in New York City. Jerry and Bea would visit Bennington every year or two.

According to Dot: "We all went to Peter and Nancy's wedding. I think of Peter as my brother-in-law. My parents thought the world of Pete as he has been a wonderful step father to my niece.

"But losing Dick left a huge hole in our family, one that could never be filled. The worst thing in the world happened to us, but we all survived in one way or another because, as my mom would say over and over, life is for the living."

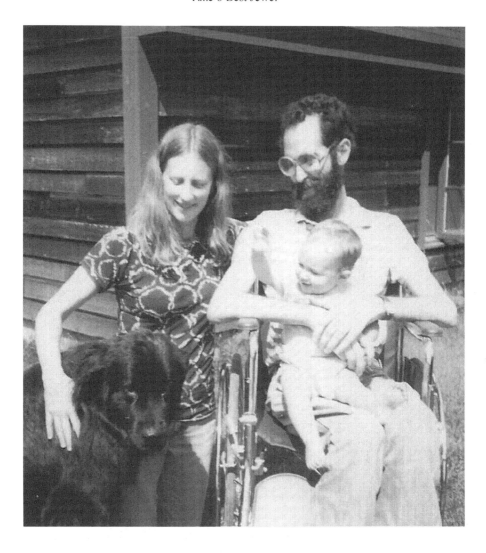

Chapter 18
Where are they now?

Jerry and Bea Barad celebrated their 68th wedding anniversary on June 24, 2014. They still lived in the same house in Hunterdon County, NJ, that they built in 1961. Jerry and Bea hosted the Succulent Society members and the curious once a year with an Open House to tour the two greenhouses, and Jerry spent much time deciding which species he would sell at the Open Houses.

Bea developed a condition called aortic stenosis which is the narrowing of the exit of the left ventricle of the heart. The condition developed over time. Her condition deteriorated in May, 2014. That June, her cardiologist suggested that an artificial heart valve might help. After the surgery, she spent some time in rehab but never fully recovered. She returned home for a few days of hospice care and died at 11:45 a.m. on August 18, 2014.

Jerry was very lonely after Bea died but his children kept in touch with him using Facebook messenger each day. Jerry called his son David on Thursday, January 14, 2016, because he was very excited that he had found his military discharge papers along with everyone's birth certificates. Later that night, he developed chest pains and called for an ambulance to take him to the Hunterdon Medical Center. David spoke with his father by phone in the ER. Jerry had suffered a heart attack and an attempt to open it with a stent had been unsuccessful.

It was decided to move Jerry to Morristown Medical Center, some 30 miles away. Bob had flown home from Africa and joined Jerry at Morristown Friday evening. David planned to join them on Saturday. Dot was in Paris, France. Bob called David early Saturday morning to tell him that Jerry had gone into cardiac arrest and that they were coding him. Bob arranged for a three-way call with David and Dot and put the phone to Jerry's ear so that each could say a short good-bye.

Jerry died soon after, at 4:35 a.m. on Saturday, January 16, 2016.

The first question the funeral director asked at the funeral home was if the kids had Jerry's discharge papers so he could have veteran's honors. This was just two days after Jerry had called

David to say he had found them. The papers were neatly placed in an envelope sitting on his kitchen table.

Jerry and Bea are buried together in adjoining plots at the Jewish Community Center cemetery in Flemington, NJ.

David Barad and Iris were married on June 20, 1974, the summer prior to when he and Dick started medical school. Dick was the best man at their wedding and the groomsmen included Fred Huber, Randy Motz, and David's college roommates Arch MacInnes and Allan Schulman. The men had what David called a "low key" bachelor party the night before the wedding, sitting around Jerry and Bea's swimming pool, drinking a few beers, and watching a meteor shower. There are pictures of Dick wearing a blue tuxedo at the wedding.

David and Iris' oldest daughter Alexis was born on June 14, 1980. Alexis is married to Jessie Cutler, a lawyer, and they have two sons: Julien was born in September, 2011, and Gavi was born in May, 2014. Alexis is a writer and worked in publishing at Random House and Harper. She is the author of the children's book *Who Are We? An Animal Guessing Game*. She also is a regular contributor to online blogs about motherhood. A Google search of her name brings up quite a few hits.

Second child Justin was born on April 24, 1984, the same year Dot gave birth to her first child Noah in June, and Nancy gave birth to Leah in October. Justin is working at FOODA in marketing and advertising. FOODA is a company that brings pop-up restaurants into places of business. He also is actively working on composing and mixing music on computers and from time to time performs as a DJ.

Youngest daughter Ashley was born October 27, 1994. She is a graduate of Vassar College having majored in Hispanic Studies and is currently working as a legal assistant in her brother-in-law Jessie's law office.

"When Alexis and Justin were born," David recalled, "Nancy and Dick gave them each a baby quilt sent down from Vermont. We always called the quilts their "Uncle Dickie" blankets. When Ashley was born, Nancy sent one down for her as well, continuing the 'Uncle Dickie blanket' tradition."

David visited Bennington frequently during the summer of

1985, but after Dick died, he did not get back there again until Leah's wedding in 2012, some 27 years later. "The wedding was a very emotional experience for me, revisiting many difficult feelings," he recalled. Nancy and Peter live in the house next door to where Nancy, Dick, and Leah lived, and this was the setting for Leah's wedding. During his visit, David and Dot took a walk next door to see the old house again which "looked much the same as it always did."

David finished his training as an OB/GYN and Reproductive Endocrinologist. He "had the pleasure" of helping to develop *in vitro* fertilization (IVF) "which did not exist when I was in medical school," he recalled. After finishing his fellowship in 1984, David became Director of Reproductive Endocrinology at Albert Einstein College of Medicine until 2003. He was an investigator in the Women's Health Initiative and headed its hormone advisory committee for many years.

In 2003, he joined the Center for Human Reproduction in Manhattan where he still works. One of his patients made a small sculpture of David and his partner dressed as magicians pulling a newborn baby out of a hat. He is very active academically, publishing 15-20 academic papers each year.

In 1996, the family moved to Closter, New Jersey, where he and Iris still live. In 2005, David was elected to the Closter Town Council and has been reelected twice since then and continues to serve on the council.

David still plays guitar occasionally. In 2013, he and Dot drove to Boston for the Bat Mitzvah of their second cousin Ann's daughter. That Saturday night there was a party at Ann's house, and David brought out his guitar and, with Dot's support, played some of the old songs that he and Dick used to play together which he felt was another way of bringing the three of them back together again, however briefly.

"I miss my brother Dick," David said. "I have missed his advice and guidance and wisdom."

Dorothy "Dot" Barad Bowers married Bruce Waterman on September 3, 1982, in a ceremony held in her parent's back yard where Dick offered the first toast to the bride and groom. Eldest son Noah Barad Waterman was born in June 26, 1984, the same year as his cousins Leah and Justin.

Dot had moved her family into her grandmother's house in Brooklyn when Dick became ill to be closer to the family. After Dick died, she felt compelled to have another child. "I felt very strongly that I needed to create something I could love after losing someone so dear," she recalled.

Second son Aaron Richard Waterman was born on February 6, 1987, and his middle name was in memory of the uncle he would never know. She sent out birth announcements, including one to Harry Bowers who she had met in the early 1970s in a class for alternative processes in photography. Bowers had his own company, Bowers Imaging Technologies (BIT) in California, at the time. When he received the birth announcement, Harry "called me on the phone saying that he had been looking for me and offered me a job at his new company," Dot remembered.

She took the job and moved her family from Brooklyn to the San Francisco Bay area in 1988. "This was the first large scale digital color printing system ever created," she recalled. "This was before color monitors or desktop scanners. It was a fascinating and exciting time working with digital technology so early in 1988."

But it also came with a cost. Her marriage to Bruce fell apart soon after arriving in the Bay area, and they divorced in the fall of 1989. Shortly after, Dot and Harry became a couple. "I had two kids under the age of five," she said.

Harry and Dot left BIT when Harry along with two partners started a company called Cactus. ("Harry said my dad would like the name," Dot said.) This was the first company to sell large format digital color printing systems using Macintosh computers and Versatec electrostatic printers. In early 1990, Harry and his son John, the company programmer, moved to New York City. Dot could not join them full time because of a custody issue concerning moving her two young children across country. So, Dot commuted back and forth between Berkeley, California, and New York City by time-sharing her job with a young woman who was attending graduate school. She commuted this way for 14 years, from 1990 until 2004. Her boys would visit New York during summers when they were not in school.

Cactus was sold to 3M in 1997. Harry then developed another software company that corrected color output from any printer to match the color on the monitor. This business was sold to ColorVision in 2000.

It was only then that Harry and Dot decided to get married, which they did on Friday, September 13, 2000. When Dot married Harry, she became step mother to Harry's two children, John Bowers and Chloe Bowers. John has two sons, Max and Fritz, and Chloe has a son, Harry, and twin girls Ruth and Sadie born in 2012. Dot describes herself as a practicing grandmother.

Dot and Harry have since purchased an atelier in Paris, France, and spend several months a year there. They also have a 42-acre farm "in the middle of nowhere" near Rhinebeck, New York.

Dot was with her mother in the Flemington home the night before Bea passed away. Earlier that day, she had found out from Nancy that Leah was pregnant. Even though Bea was in and out of consciousness that night, Dot kept saying to Bea, "Mama, Leah is expecting a baby." She said this over and over without getting a response. Suddenly, Bea's eyes opened and she smiled a broad smile and said, "Leah is expecting a baby!" She died the following morning but Dot has always felt blessed that her mother had found a moment of happiness in those bleak hours.

Dot was in Paris with Harry when Jerry suffered his heart attack. He died before she could get home. For a few days after his funeral, Dot and Bob were snowed in at their parents' house and they began sorting out the important things found in Jerry's office. Dot spent most of that year taking care of the living things: placing Jerry's beloved cats Kiber and Moose in good homes; distributing his cactus and succulent collection to collectors and botanical gardens; moving his koi pond to her own pond in Rhinebeck, NY; and helping guide Derek, who was a full-time helper with all of Jerry's gardens and plants, into the Professional Gardner program at Longwood Gardens.

Dot always made it a point to keep her sons and Leah connected and made many visits to Bennington with them during the summer vacations. "This built a very strong connection between the cousins," she said, "and they are close in a way that I know Dick would have loved."

Dot and Nancy have remained very close. "Nancy is one of my closest friends," she said. "She is my sister. I think of her husband Pete as my brother-in-law." Dot attempts to get to Bennington at least twice a year, and Nancy and Pete make the trip to Rhinebeck when they can.

"If kicking and screaming could have changed anything about Dick, we all would still be kicking and screaming," she said. "But as my mom always says, 'Life is for the living,' and Dick would have expected us to live it to our maximum.

"I miss him. That will never change."

Robert "Bob" Barad did his undergraduate work at Columbia University in New York City where he earned a B.A. in History and Political Science in 1980. He went on to American University in Washington, D.C. where he earned his law degree (J.D.) from the AU's Washington School of Law in 1986, and then his M.A. in International Relations and African Studies from the AU School of Social Sciences in 1988.

He met Nancy Zlotsky in Brattleboro, Vermont, in 1982 while they were both attending a program at the School for International Training. Nancy had grown up in Tolland, Connecticut. They were married in 1986 and had two sons: Richard Zlotsky Barad (named after his uncle) born June 23, 1992, in Washington, D.C., a recent graduate of George Washington University with a B.A. in Geography and Geographic Information Systems; and Sam Zlotsky Barad, born December 30, 1996, in Washington, D.C., who is learning disabled with autism and attends a residential school for children with special needs in Massachusetts.

Bob is an international civil servant who has worked for the United Nations World Food Programme since 1997. He began his career in IT services, worked more recently as a speechwriter in the Office of the Executive Director, and is now a Regional Programme Officer for the West Africa Bureau. He has been stationed in Dakar, Senegal since July, 2013.

His son Richard lived in Ivory Coast and Uganda from ages 4 through 12, then moved with Bob to Rome, Italy. Richard's Bar Mitzvah took place in Rome in July, 2005. The event was well-attended by both Zlotsky and Barad family members and included a Barad family reunion with Jackie Herbert and the first opportunity for them to meet Jackie's daughter Jo.

Nancy Scattergood Donavan still lives in Bennington, Vermont, in the house next door to where she lived with Dick. Pete and his wife Sally Donavan were their neighbors at the time of Dick's passing. Sally and Pete separated in 1986, then divorced the following year. Nancy and Pete "connected" and they ended up getting married on August 26, 1989. Nancy and Leah moved into Pete's house next door. About six months after Pete and Nancy married, Pete adopted Leah.

Nancy stayed with Bennington Family Practice until 1995 and then bought an office building in Bennington and went "solo" until 2007. She worked part time for a Dartmouth/Hitchcock group practice in Manchester, Vermont., and retired in August, 2015.

Interestingly, the family doctor who replaced Dick at Bennington Family Practice about a year after Dick died, John Hearst, had trained in the same residency program in Wisconsin with Dick and Nancy. He bought the house where Dick died from Nancy in 1989 and lived there for many years. His daughter Jory became Leah's best friend and was the maid of honor at Leah's wedding, where John officiated (as is possible to do in Vermont, he secured a license to perform Leah and Eric's marriage in Bennington). When John's marriage dissolved, they sold the house.

Nancy is fully retired now, volunteering some but staying busy with her gardening and sewing and playing bridge. Pete sold his agency "Wills Insurance" in January, 2016, and is also fully retired. They spend most of the winter months in South Carolina.

Nancy makes the trip to the cemetery to visit Dick's grave on three specific occasions each year: April 21 (his birthday), May 29 (their anniversary), and September 24 (the date of his death).

Leah Barad attended Cornell University, as her dad had done. She began her studies in Psychology in September, 2003, and met her husband, Eric Brumer, in the spring of 2004 when he became her linear algebra tutor. They graduated together in the spring, 2007, and Eric got a job with Microsoft which meant moving to Seattle, Washington. Leah had no other plans, so she moved there with him.

Leah and Eric got married in July, 2012, in Bennington, Vermont. They currently live in the Seattle area. Leah has her own photography company, LeahB Photography, (www.leahb.com), which would come as no surprise to her father.

Their son, Nathan Richard Brumer, was born on April 3, 2015. His middle name is in honor of his grandfather, Dick. "Everyone says he has my father's ears," Leah said.

She tries to get back to Bennington at least twice a year, but admits she doesn't always make the trip over to the Park Lawn Cemetery to visit her father's grave. When she does go, however, she takes along a few Oreos and leaves them on the grave as some people leave rocks or flowers.

"I wouldn't say his actual grave has ever been an important spot for me," she wrote. "Instead, I think about him just being everywhere. I talk to him when I'm upset or scared. I guess (the way) some people might pray, I talk to my father. Other ways I think about him that you might find interesting...I have his Cornell ID card in my wallet. On his death day, I always light a candle and pull out a stack of letters he wrote to me or others wrote about him after his death. Daffodils are my favorite flower and always remind me of him."

Jackie Herbert Marks would prefer to keep the details of her current life private, but she has led a happy life, has enjoyed a career in fashion design, was married, has a family, paints, and currently lives in Herefordshire, England.

Epilogue

From a poster that hung in Jackie Herbert's house for many years.

Sonnet 65

Since brass, nor stone, nor earth, nor boundless sea,
But sad mortality o'er-sways their power,
How with this rage shall beauty hold a plea,
Whose action is no stronger than a flower?
O, how shall summer's honey breath hold out
Against the wreckful siege of battering days,
When rocks impregnable are not so stout,
Nor gates of steel so strong, but Time decays?
O fearful meditation! where, alack,
Shall Time's best jewel from Time's chest lie hid?
Or what strong hand can hold his swift foot back?
Or who his spoil of beauty can forbid?
    O, none, unless this miracle have might,
    That in black ink my love may still shine bright.

- William Shakespeare

Postscript
by Wayne Dilts

It was Dot's brief comments at the Class of 1970 reunion in the fall of 2010 that struck me so powerfully, that Dick confessed to her that he was afraid he would be forgotten. Those words echoed in my head for the next ten weeks after the reunion until I finally got up the nerve to send David and Dot an email in January, 2011:

Hi-

Would you be averse to my writing Dick's biography? It would mean that I would ask you, often, to write out your personal remembrances. Ultimately, I'd like to turn it into a book. I think his story is a remarkable one that should be preserved, but I couldn't do it without your permission and cooperation. Let me know what you think.....just a thought at this point...

Dot responded the next day:

I have no objection but will have to ask Nancy Dick's wife if she has any feelings about this too. I will be back in touch.
hugs
D

The day after that, David responded:

OK Dot... I was thinking about this (intermittently) all weekend. This is something I often thought of doing myself... so having Wayne organize it will be easier than trying to parse out the stories ourselves. So... I am in. We should probably enlist Mom and Dad and Jackie as well... to get all perspectives.
D

And so, as is said, the die was cast and we were off. I got very supportive emails from Dick's wife, Nancy, and a heart-warming note from his daughter, Leah, encouraging me. It was Leah that really put it in perspective for me: she never knew her father, and had been hungry to hear stories about him all her life (see Appendix A).

This then became a much more personal project than I had planned, for I realized that I would be preserving Dick's memory not only for the family and friends that knew him, but for the one person in this world who wanted to know him best and actually knew him the least, his daughter.

All the members of the Barad family opened their hearts and memories to me without hesitation. I know that remembering some of these events brought smiles and even out-loud laughter, but I also realize that some of the most painful memories were also ones that were necessary to revisit. I cannot thank them enough for their thoughtfulness and even the bravery it took to share some of those stories with me. They allowed me to pry into their lives as no one ever has before, and I appreciate their trust.

Dick died when he was 33, and this is 30+ years later that we are trying to remember. So, some events, names, and dates remain fuzzy. If there are any corrections to be made to this text, I take full responsibility for their presentation here. I pressed the family members and friends for as much information as I could get; they were remarkable in what they could include, but with the passage of so much time and memories dimming as they have for all of us, it was impossible to recapture everything.

But what I set out to do was capture the essence of the man.

Pulitzer Prize-winning author John Matteson wrote in his biography *The Lives of Margaret Fuller* (2012) a warning that writing a memoir of someone who died young, as Margaret Fuller tragically did, is fraught with the danger of wanting to present the deceased in the most enviable of lights.

"A(n)...historical challenge presented by a subject who died young is the tendency of the subject's biographers...to hallow and sanctify the memory of the departed. The first light that is turned on such a subject often creates a distorting halo."

Because of the title I chose for this book, I thought I might be guilty of that "tendency." My working title had been "The Brightest Crayon in the Box," an immediate jump to that hallowed ground of beatifying the memory of my friend - because Dick was the brightest person I have ever known. But that title gave way to the one I use here when I read the Shakespearean sonnet that had hung on Jackie's wall for many years.

So, I am not pandering to Dick's memory in calling him "Time's Best Jewel." It is the best way to describe him. I didn't create a halo effect around Dick: he did it himself. There was no "dark" side. He was the same person to everyone who met him.

He was a confluence of good: he worked hard to become the best he could be, he loved deeply, cared passionately, treated humanity with respect and love, fought and worked for the underdog and the less fortunate, believed that people in need needed to be helped, and that people of means had an obligation to help.

He cared.

That was just the way he lived.

Time's Best Jewel?

You bet.

Appendices

The following are a collection of emails, articles, and writings by and about members of the Barad family that contribute to their family history. Not all of these are strictly about Dick.

Appendix A
E-mail to Wayne Dilts from Leah Barad

January 22, 2011
Hi Wayne,

My name is Leah Barad and I am Dick Barad's daughter. My mom, Nancy, forwarded me the string of emails you've been writing with my Aunt Dot and her about writing my father's biography. I have to say that the concept feels like a special gift to me, I mean who more than the daughter that never knew him would want to read about his life?

Sadly, I have no stories to share, as I was only 11 months old when he died, but I thought you might be interested in some of the things I've written about him in my own quest to get to know him better. I think I did most of my soul searching between 12th grade and college, which also happened to be the time where I was asked to write various assignments that seemed to fit right in. The first attachment is a section of an Autobiography I wrote for one of my 12th grade English Classes. The second is an essay I wrote for my Cornell Application. The question was to pick a quote and write about it and I chose a quote my father wrote in a letter to me before he died. And finally, a piece I wrote for a Freshman Year writing class at Cornell, called the "History of Cornell." The assignment was to research a deceased Cornell Alum by finding their folder in the Deceased Alumni File. We were given a list of famous alumni to look up, but I asked if I could do it on my father.

I've never been an avid writer, I prefer to express myself with a camera, but I think some of my best writing came out when thinking about my father. I think it's wonderful that you want to write a book about him and I hope the book comes to fruition. Whether it is published or not, it would make me unbelievably happy if you would share your work with me. As you'll see from what I have written over the years, I've spent a lot of time thinking about him and wanting to know him. It always makes me happy when I meet old friends and hear old stories.

I wish you the best of luck and please let me know if I can be of any help!

Leah

Leah's 12th grade English essay

Autobiography: My Father

In my Catholic elementary school, they taught us to pray to God before bed each night. This never made much sense to me, but I did not want to disobey my teachers, so I would stare out though my skylight each night and babble away the thoughts of the day. I'd ask questions, imagining the answers not that God would give me but those that would come from my father. I'll admit that I felt guilty for not doing exactly as my teachers directed me, but I decided that it was close enough. Maybe it was something my mother told me - maybe it was something I picked up from books or movies - but as I talked, I would single out the brightest star and imagine him looking down on me.

My uncle asked me once if I remember when I first understood that my father had died. I was 11 months when the cancer caught up with him, too young to remember his face, his touch, his voice, anything. It's been a fact of life, like someone saying that they have two brothers, I have no biological father. I even bragged about it in preschool. "Your daddy's a lawyer? Well, mine *died*." It made me different from the other kids. Sometime in my early elementary school years, my attitude changed. I honestly think that one day I sat down and decided to shut up about it. When I do tell people about his death, I squint my eyes then watch as they wipe the smile from their face and exclaim how sorry they are. I shrug my shoulders. I'm sorry, too.

He was a great man. At least that's what I imagine. At least that's what I've been told. On the day I was born, he skipped around the hospital where he worked announcing how beautiful and wonderful his daughter was. I always liked that story. I see in him a fun-loving spirit, always ready to laugh, always ready listen. I see a sparkle in his eyes and skip in his step. Care in his voice and gentleness in his touch. There is nothing about him that annoys me. He's perfect.

There is so much I don't know.

I want to ask my grandmother about him, about his childhood, his likes, his dislikes. I invited her up to my room once. She walked in, glanced at my walls and immediately turned back towards the stairs. I followed behind. "Grandma, you didn't get to see the whole room." She turned, looked me straight in the eye, and then continued down. I stood frozen. Her eyes were filled with water, her cheeks damp. I went back in my room and stood exactly where she had. A picture of her son, my father, hung above the bed, another on the bureau, and another on the desk. That was eight years ago. There is so much I could have asked in eight years.

Sometimes I get an email from my aunt describing some memory of him. It's as if she just needs to let it roll off her mind. She's told me stories that have made me laugh and smile and wish so desperately that he could hold my hand and tell me the tales himself. I love those emails, but I could never ask her to speak about him; I have to wait for the times she needs to talk.

After his death, my mom threw some of his stuff in a trunk. This summer we went through it together and cleaned it out for the first time. She hadn't been able to part with anything, not even the mold of his orthotics; but now, seventeen years later it was easy for her to sort the clothes and papers into keep, throw, and giveaway piles. She told me stories of when he wore "that jacket" or "those pants." She would point out his favorite articles of clothing and I'd put them aside for myself. I found a box of letters, some written to him, some condolences, some written by him. I went through each one, absorbing the way he wrote or the way others wrote about him.

Then I found it. A letter he wrote to me. It was my mom's handwriting, as he was too sick to write at the time but they were his words. The only words he ever wrote directly to me. "Be wise, know yourself, and have a good life. I did, it was just too short." I dropped the card. I cried. I picked the card up again. He said this?

Sitting next to the open trunk with my mom, I asked questions I'd been too afraid to ask before. I want to know more about this man, this man who called himself my "daddy." I want to know his habits, his likes, his dislikes; I want to know him. I bounce my leg when I sit, I move my hands in a specific way, and I wonder if I inherited these traits. I've often caught his family members studying me, looking for him inside a different body. I won't ever be him, I won't ever truly know him; I just hope that what I am would have made him proud.

Leah's Cornell application essay

"Be wise, know yourself, and have a good life. I did, it was just too short."

The first time I read these lines I cried. They were the last words of a birthday card my father wrote to me just days before he died from brain cancer. I found the letter this summer as I rummaged through a trunk of clothes, papers, and knickknacks that my mom had saved after his death. I was almost one then, and now as I begin my nineteenth year, my curiosity about him grows stronger. I want to know his habits, his likes, his dislikes. I want to know him.

Growing up I've heard stories that have made me laugh and smile and wish so desperately that he could hold my hand and tell me the tales himself. Comments in his old yearbooks, condolence letters, and stories, depict him as a leader, a faithful friend, and caring brother, someone who was always ready to laugh and always ready to help another in need. I absorb these descriptions and hope that I have had the fortune of inheriting such wonderful traits. I would be beyond proud for his family to tell me that I reminded them of him.

Sometimes I lie awake at night and talk to him. I ask him for guidance; how to deal with stress, how to help a friend. Recently, when I've wanted to talk to him, his first and last bit of advice has popped into my head. "Be wise," he says. Though wisdom can come in many forms, I imagine that he is asking me to do what I know is right, whether that be concerning my friends and family or myself. I have always been dubbed "the good kid." I do what my parents tell me and stay out of trouble. I have put enough pressure on myself to keep up the grades and accomplish all my tasks that my parents have never had to force me to do it. My mom often tells me that the death of my father has made me very astute to the feelings of others. I refuse to make a decision without knowing how it might affect those around me and I cannot stand to see people upset.

To be truly wise you must be able to follow your heart, to "know yourself". It is through my family, my friends, and even my acquaintances that I have learned the most about myself. They have been my laughter, my support, and my teachers. It is because of them that I've found my independence; it is because of them that I've found my self-confidence. They challenge my ideas and help me to refine my own thoughts and opinions.

Above all, my friends and family have taught me to make the best out of all situations, to "have a good life". I know it's not plausible to be happy at every moment, but no matter how bad a time I am having I try to slap on a smile and remind myself of what's important. One of the greatest lessons I have learned is that sometimes it is better to sit and talk with a friend or go to sleep than it is to finish that last homework assignment. You need to know when to be serious and when to relax and have fun, because, as my father reminds me, our time is finite; we truly need to make what we have worth it.

When I first read the letter, I could not believe that it was actually written by him. All my life I had wondered what he might say to me if he ever had the chance, and here it was, advice, written directly from him to me. I have read it to the point that I can recite the words without looking at the card. He tells me that he regrets not being able to watch me grow and become an adult. I can only hope that the person I have become and will continue to be would have made him proud.

Leah's paper on a deceased Cornell alumni   2/29/04

Richard Michael Barad

In the early 1970s, Richard Michael Barad attended Cornell University. He spent his time studying, trying to figure out his future, hiking around Cayuga Lake, and spending time with friends. His roommate, Bill Johnson, and Bill's girlfriend, Billy-Jo, all but took over his dorm room freshman year. He accredits his high GPA to the hours they forced him to spend in the library. After freshman year, he moved into an apartment with three close friends on Hudson Street. Like most undergraduates, he absentmindedly filled out information cards each year and come senior year refused to pose for the *Cornellian* because it was the *uncool* thing to do. At least that's the story of my father's Cornell experience that I have pieced together. How was that young, dark curly-haired man with an easy smile to know that thirty years later, his daughter, with the same dark curly hair, would be attending the same university and looking up his name in the deceased alumni folders?

When told that the Cornell archives kept records of deceased alumni, I froze. I had wondered where I could find records of my father's existence at this school, but with the opportunity placed in front of me I did not know what to do. I have spent countless hours contemplating what my life would be like if he had not died when I was eleven months old. Would I be in the same place? Would I be the same person? Perhaps I'd still attend Cornell, though doubtless for different reasons. I constantly grasp at ways to learn about my father, but each time something new presents itself, such as the archives, I have to take a deep breath and work up the courage to go after it.

Too nervous to go alone, I pulled a good friend down to the archives to hold my hand. My chest tightened as I picked up pieces of paper that he had filled out years ago. The contents of the folder provided me with little information that I did not already know but I couldn't stop staring at his handwriting. Like so many of the things Mom has given me of his, I sat and held the piece of paper, awestruck that once upon a time he had sat and held the same parchment.

Even though I knew that he did not have a picture in the 1974 *Cornellian* I insisted on looking through the yearbook to get a sense of what the university was like when he attended. Flipping through the pages it stuck me how similar everything seemed. My father could easily have hung out on the lawn outside of Donlon, just like I have done numerous times. He could have sat in Uris library and distractedly scanned over the same book titles I peruse when I cannot keep my mind focused on my work. He could have sat in the same lecture halls and possibly listened to the same professor. Whenever an acquaintance mentions that their parents went to Cornell, I quickly ask them the year, desperate to find someone that knew my father. Perhaps they could tell me exactly what he did while he was here, and perhaps I would be able to say I have done the same things.

People have always told me that my father loved Cornell and I cannot help but constantly wonder what exactly made his life here so wonderful. Most days I go about my daily business like any Cornell undergrad: hanging out with friends, getting my work done, and going to class. Sometimes, however, I will recall that my father used to walk down these same paths and my actions will no longer be about being a college student, they will be about retracing my father's steps, about finding him in a place he loved.

Everything I have known about my father is through stories, but by attending Cornell I have created a way for me to learn about him for myself. I often imagine that the Cornell culture that my father experienced and the one in which I am now immersed are almost the same, enough so that I can feel that by being here I am sharing an experience with him. Each day I walk around Cornell's vast campus I feel my father's presence among the hustle of college life; sometimes, it's almost as if I could reach out and touch him. I may never have known Richard Michael Barad, but he is very much a part of me and all that I do. I go through each day, walking through the same buildings as he did, up the same hills, and in the same dormitories, happy to be at Cornell and happy to have found a connection with my father.

Barad, Richard Michael. DAF, Rare Manuscripts Collection. Kroch library, Cornell University.

Appendix B

Leah's Wedding, July 14, 2012
Bennington, Vermont

As remembered by Dot:

The wedding was lovely, hot but lovely. Eric's mother is an event planner from Montreal so the tent, the catering and the music were all brought down from there.... Very, very upscale.

The trip to the cemetery was very emotional. My parents had not been to Bennington in many, many years. The same for David and his children. Nancy and I had planted sunflowers together during my last visit and they were blooming. Sunflowers were also part of the wedding theme.

I brought up to Bennington a bag of Oreo cookies, Dick's favorites, and we all shared cookies at the grave site. My Dad asked me to sing a song that was "my song" when I was three. My grandmother taught it to me and I sang it at her funeral. I guess I will be singing it a few more times in the future as it has now a different status in the way I feel about it.... if that makes sense. I left three cookies on Dick's grave, kind of a variation of the stones we Jews leave to show you have visited a grave. Jews don't leave flowers and I do not remember why.

The hardest points of the wedding were the places where Dick should have been: the walk down the aisle on her father's arm, and the father/daughter dance. Pete, Nancy's husband who also adopted Leah, is such a special guy and was wonderful, but that had little to do with the pain I felt/we felt collectively. During the dance, I was folded around my Mom holding her close. I looked at my son Noah on the other side of the table and he mouthed to me I should pick up my phone. He had sent me a text message: he thought it would call too much attention if he stood up and walked over to me but he wanted to let me know he wished he was holding me in his arms.

Leah and Eric gave a lot of thought to symbolically including many things to hold all the families together. One touch was that their wedding cake was decorated with Oreo cookies, which was very sweet of them and heartfelt meaningful.

Nancy looked lovely. And it was great to see some of her extended family who I have always felt close to but don't get to see very often. Her mom Jean is such a character who I am very fond of. Mom always says Jean is her favorite in-law. Nancy's youngest brother, Kirk, is a close friend of mine. He attended my wedding to my first husband but lives in Wisconsin and I had never met his now-grown daughters. It was Kirk's wedding that Nancy flew to on a private charter plane just days before Dick passed away. I stayed with Dick in Bennington so she could attend with baby Leah.

Life is made of moments and this past weekend was one of the markers in a life. It was great my parents were able to be there and my brother Bob, too.

Appendix C

The Opal

Dot: When Dick was dying, Nancy had him pick out a ring to give Leah on her sixteenth birthday. I was amazed in the middle of all this that she was able to think that clearly. Sadly, the ring was lost while she was in college... but hey it was the thought that mattered at that moment.

This is the email exchange from my parents to Nancy a few months after Leah's 16th birthday.

(On April 12, 2001, Nancy sent the following note to Dick's father & mother.)
From: Peter & Nancy Donavan
To: Gerald Barad MD
Subject: FW: The opal

Hi, I thought that you might like to see what Leah is writing in school. I think that the assignment was to write a sonnet. Love, Nancy

The Opal

A golden ring around my finger lies,
Pale-bright colors swirl, an eye to the past.
A treasure given as a father dies,
Along with the questions I've always asked.

The circuit continues, coiled and curled
Around my finger and mind it does spin,
The more you reflect the further you're twirled,
The end is the same as where you begin.

All I envision is that golden prize.
Memories never experienced flash,
But none can I witness with my own eyes,
Though they stay with me 'til the very last.

The ring is clouded by the constant sound
Of memories always, but never quite round.

(Dr. Barad replied)

From: Gerald Barad
Sent: Sunday, April 15, 2001
To: 'Peter & Nancy Donavan'
Subject: RE: The opal

Dear Nancy and Peter,
The years do fly by! I remember so very well when you told us that
Dick had bought a ring to give to Leah when she was sixteen. I had
always wondered how Leah responded to this little gift from Dick
but somehow I was unable to ask. Now I have my answer. Bea and
I were deeply touched by Leah's sonnet and I am afraid we did
shed a few tears. You and Peter have done so much to keep Dick's
memory alive and we are so grateful.
We love you all so much.
Mom and Dad

(Then he sent the following note to Dot.)

From: Gerald Barad
To: Barad, Dot
Subject: FW: The opal
Date: Mon, 16 Apr 2001

Nancy's note to me and my reply. Don't cry, we love you. Dad

Appendix D

The ad Dick Barad placed in The Hunterdon County Democrat in 1969 in support of the referendum to lower the voting age to 18 in New Jersey

The November 4th election will pose to the voters of New Jersey a major decision concerning the future of the youth of this state. The decision made will strongly affect the outcome in 12 other states where similar constitutional amendments will be put up before ballot next year. The youth of our state are standing up to meet the decision of the voting public. We are not demanding the right to choose our policies and policy makers; we are sincerely requesting the highly-esteemed privilege of voting. We are asking for the chance to prove our honest concern and maturity.

Ours is a generation of great awareness. Being part of the television age and a revolutionary society has brought about deep realization of national and international affairs in early adulthood. With decisions about future professions and jobs thrust upon us by the age of 16 it is a necessity to attain goals and ideals.

The privilege of voting at eighteen is not a shining star to us merely because it is there and to be gained. The need for a voice in government is felt because we hold a genuine concern for and belief in our nation; its heritage and our future.
The world is right on top of us – we live with it at our front door every day.

It is our hope that our maturity and ability to accept responsibility has been realized by you – the voter. We hope to gain your vote in our favor through sincere effort and intelligent organization. Not by loud demands and senseless riots. We are uniting in an organized plea for public support.

It is not by our efforts alone that this bill will be passed. Our campaign and encouragement is worthless without the support of the New Jersey voter. Believe in youth and give us a chance.

Ordered and paid for by the Hunterdon Central High School Student Council, Richard Barad, president, Flemington N.J.

.

Appendix E

Dick Barad's letter to the Editor of The Hunterdon County Democrat, November, 1969

I'd like to make a plea to all the voters of this county, through this letter, to trust the youth of our state.

I'd like to ask the voters to approve the referendum which would give the right to vote to all citizens between 18 and 21 years of age.

The "magic" of the number 21 is straight from the Middle Ages. A man of that age could fight and own land. If one could do these things he, as a result, had some influence in politics.

The Renaissance came in the 15th and 16th centuries and many of the old ways of the Dark Ages changed. The "magic" of the age 21, however, is still with us.

Today's youth are the involved generation. I need only to point to the many members of my student council for examples of citizens concerned and involved in the affairs of their community, state, and country.

Citizens under 21 are fighting and dying for our country. The fact that they have the ability to fight at 18 does not qualify them to vote. However, they should have some say in the affairs of the country for which they fight and die.

When you vote, realize that there is a large number of citizens who have the intelligence to vote but are yet denied the privilege. Realize that every age group has extremists and those who wish to escape. Think of those young people you know personally.

The major educators of our state, the two candidates for governor, our present governor, and the President of the United State support lowering the voting age.

Have faith in the youth of our state.

Richard Barad, President
Hunterdon Central High School Student Council

Appendix F

The list of school activities Richard M. Barad participated in while as a student at Hunterdon Central High School, as found in the Echo 70, the HCHS yearbook, page 166. The numbers 1, 2, 3, 4 represent which year in high school he participated:

Band: 1, 2, 3, 4
Track 1, 2, 3, 4
Interact Club 1, 2, junior director 3, President 4
Student Council 2, 3, President 4
Devil's Cabaret 2
Musical 2
Political Science Club President 3
Junior Class Play 3
Prom Committee Chairman 3
Boy's State Delegate 3
National Honor Society 3, 4

Appendix G

Dick's Personal Statement when applying to Residency Programs

Personal Statement – Richard M. Barad

It is difficult to encapsulate those factors in my life that are most pertinent to this statement. The following thoughts, however, come to mind.

I was born in New York City in 1952, while my father was a medical student at Cornell. He continued his medical training by completing a residency in OB/GYN at Bellevue Hospital. It was in 1957, when I was five years old, that my mother and father, both raised in Brooklyn, took their young family, my brother David two years older than I, Dorothy two years younger, and myself (Bobby, the youngest, wouldn't be coming along for another two years), to a small rural community, Hunterdon County, N.J. There, my father became Director of OB/GYN at the then three years old Hunterdon Medical Center. My formative years were spent in Hunterdon County and the health care system to which I was exposed has been called the Hunterdon Plan. Hunterdon is a rural community in which nearly all of the primary care is provided by Family Physicians with appropriate specialty consultation and referral. Hunterdon was one of the 1st institutions in this country to recognize a need to produce well trained general physicians, and one of the 1st Family Practice Residencies was established there in 1969. HMC has become recognized nationally for its delivery of quality and cost-effective health care. In terms of "role models", growing up in Hunterdon provided both a model of health care delivery and of the Family Physician as the foundation of that delivery system. This model has stood out in bold contrast to the delivery of medical care as I've now experienced it in my medical training thus far.

I was educated in public schools through high school. In 1970 I went to Cornell University, majoring in Biological Sciences, however, with a broad-based education including the humanities and social sciences. It was there that I made the decision to go into medicine, with the major differential being teaching.

I entered Rutgers Medical School in 1974. Aside from my

academic exposure to basic sciences at Rutgers, I was able to take part in several elective and summer experiences, which added to my understanding of family practice and my desire to do primary care. As a first year student, I took part in an elective entitled "Introduction to the Patient" in which two afternoons a month were spent in a family practitioner's office. In the summer following my first year, I spent eight weeks working as an extern investigating child abuse and neglect with the New Jersey Division of Youth and Family Services.

My second year provided an opportunity to take an elective in ER Medicine in which two evenings per month were spent learning "1st contact – primary care" as it presents in a hospital ER. Near the end of the second year at Rutgers, myself and five other students approached the Dept. of Family Practice concerning the lack of an opportunity for students at Rutgers to get clinical exposure to Family Practice, prior to the time when career choices must be made. From this initiative, a discussion group was formed which resulted in the creation of a summer family practice preceptorship program. Under this program I spent 6 weeks in a preceptorship at the Phillips-Barbour Family Health Center, the model unit for the residency program at Hunterdon. This experience, more than any other, solidifies my ideas about family practice, as I had the chance to spend time with people actively involved in the field and also envision myself in that role.

Following my second year at Rutgers, I transferred to the Albert Einstein College of Medicine. Because of a shortage of adequate clinical facilities, Rutgers has transferred out at least ½ of its class since the school began. I decided to take the opportunity to transfer so that my third and fourth years could be spent at a large urban medical center. There have been occasions over the past year when I have questioned my decision, however, I feel the move to Einstein has been a good one for at least the following reasons: 1. The involvement, as a student, in a wide range of clinical problems. 2. Exposure to the health care problems of the urban poor, especially in dealing with a hospital based health care system. 3. Exposure to "negative role models" in which human beings appear valued only for the pathology they represent. In sum, all of these factors have in part confirmed my desire to become a family physician.

On a more personal level, I might characterize myself as a somewhat reserved, friendly person and in general I like people and in turn I am liked by them. My interests include bicycling, running, tennis, photography, cooking and guitar. My brother, Dave, is a pretty good banjo picker, and he and I have had a lot of fun performing Country and Bluegrass music, in which I variously join in on guitar, washtub base [sic], harmonica, and with the vocals.

My most important personal involvement has been with my fiancée, Nancy Scattergood. Nancy is also a fourth year student at Einstein and applying for a residency in Family Practice. She and I met three years ago at Rutgers and transferred together to Einstein. The most important factor in both our lives is for us to stay together and we expect to be married prior to the beginning of our residencies in July 1978. This information is particularly pertinent to this personal statement to inform you that Nancy and I will be attempting to match together for a residency program. Under the rules provided by the NIRMP for married and engaged couples, we will be attempting to gain acceptance to a residency program prior to the match next March. If for some reason you feel that you would be unable to accept a couple under any circumstances, we hope that you would inform us of this fact prior to our interview. If, however, you are willing to consider our applications together, we would like to arrange our interviews on the same day and would be willing to be interviewed together if you consider this appropriate.

Richard M. Barad

Appendix H

Among papers that Nancy kept was a letter of recommendation for Dick from Dr. Jess Schessel from the Montefiore Hospital Medical Group in the Bronx that Dr. Schessel sent to the University of Madison. His description of Dick as a medical student is priceless.

November 14, 1977

Department of Family Medicine and Practice
777 South Mills Street
Madison, Wisconsin 53715

Dear Sir:

I am writing this letter in reference to Richard M. Barad who is applying for a Family Practice Residency in your institution.

I got to know Richard Barad during his third year pediatric clinical clerkship. I was his preceptor and met with him and with two other students two hours, three times a week.

Richard is a very receptive student. He contributed a great deal to the group. He is very bright, and was the obvious leader among the students. He is a very warm person, somewhat quiet and serious and he is a gentleman. He knows his limitations and is very honest about his ability. It was heartening to see a young man who was so anxious to learn and so sincere about wanting to take care of people.

I know Richard will be an excellent house officer and an excellent physician. It is a pleasure to recommend him to your institution.

Yours truly,
Jess Schessel, M. D

Appendix I

David Barad's speech at the Hunterdon Central High School Class of 1970 Reunion – October 30, 2010

Dick was my little brother, gone now 25 years. I'm sure he would have loved to have been with you today. Let me fill you in on what you might not have known. Dick attended Cornell as an undergraduate and went on to attend Rutgers Medical School. I spent two years in graduate school before medical school and as a result we were both in the same class, for two years. At Rutgers Dick met his lovely wife Nancy and after two years Dick and Nancy transferred out of Rutgers to Albert Einstein. They married at Nancy's family farm in south Jersey and went on to complete a family practice residency in Wisconsin. Dick and Nancy spent a year in Sierra Leone working at a mission hospital. When they returned to the U.S. they chose rural Bennington, Vermont, to live. They started a successful medical practice.

A few years later Dick developed a headache in September (1983) on Rosh Hashanah and it turned out to be brain cancer. He underwent an operation at Mass General Hospital in Boston and underwent radiation treatment there. He came home to our folks for Thanksgiving that year. He continued to recover and returned to work.

Nancy became pregnant and gave birth to their lovely daughter Leah (October 1984). In the spring of 1985 Dick experienced some back pain while jogging. His brain cancer had reoccurred. He was evaluated but could only be offered palliative treatment. That summer we had a large gathering of friends and family at their house in Vermont. He was in great pain but was well enough to try to play harmonica while I played guitar.

In September,1985, as I returned from services on the eve of Yom Kippur I received a call from Nancy that Dick was dead. I have not attended services on Yom Kippur eve since that time.

I still think of Dick almost every day. It was 25 years ago that I last saw my brother Dick, but I still see him every day. I see him when I look in the mirror, when I look at the sky and catch sight of a shooting star. I used to call him for advice. He used to call me. I still feel his presence, but I am forgetting the sound of his voice.

Dick was one of the wisest people I ever knew.

I think if he had lived he might have competed with his medical school classmate Howard Dean in Vermont politics.

I think if he had lived I would have benefitted from his insights.

I miss playing guitar and singing with him.

I miss sledding in the cold winter snow with him.

I miss him.

Appendix J

The following are excerpts of my interview with David Barad, April 12, 2012 – New York City

David: (In his autobiography) Samuel Clemens struggles in the first 200 pages of the book with the notion of biography in general, which is why he chose to publish it 100 years after his death.... He talks about what we remember about ourselves is, he says the stories that he tells are 10% based on a kernel of purely golden truth and 90% based on embroidery, not even purposeful embroidery, just based on memory. Dick's been gone a long time now so a lot of what we have is based on that embroidery and also the tendency to enhance the memory of somebody you love.

Dick was somebody who had a pretty clear vision of how he felt the world was. He had a pretty good spot in the family – somewhat protected by his older brother but still having the younger sister to take the flack for being youngest. Bobby didn't come along until much later. As I told you before, Dick and I were kind of a dyad for a long time. He was born when I was two years old, so for a long time....my memories, as far back as I can go, had Dick in them for as long as we were together. My experience was it was more like being twins with somebody who was always there as far as my conscious memory was concerned.

Dick was kind of independent but he was able to do what he chose to do. He was more likely to not necessarily follow everything that someone might ask him to do... and so, he tended to be independent from an early time. There was a time when I was the oldest and Mom would leave us together with me supervising the younger brother and sister and Mom said at one point when she was leaving, "David, if he just acts up just kick him," and Dick turned around and said, "He will not," and he kicked me. (Laughs.)

For the most part we kind of worked together on things. When we were kids, living in Ringoes, Dad had a couple of little garden plots outside. He would say, "Weed the peas while I'm at the hospital. I'll be back at 11." So, we had to go weed the peas, and this was after we fed the goats and the sheep. So, I would try to get somebody to enlist him to help us do that, so we'd end up doing it as sort of a race. He'd do one row, I'd do the other row, and we'd have a race to see who could do it the fastest. And that would work. And sometimes I'd use the technique of, "You could either weed the peas or you could shovel the manure out of the barn. Which would you rather do?" For a while you could get him to do things that way, but when we got older and he was in high school, he'd be a little harder to rouse out of bed in the morning. He was a late sleeper. Sometimes, when it came to feeding the goats, I'd get up and feed them myself because I couldn't get him out of bed and washed up in time to go down and do that.

He was very serious about his school work whereas I was a little bit more prone to social pressures, doing things around the house, doing things for Dad, and stuff like that. He was more likely to be focused and sitting at his desk and work through the afternoon working on homework. I don't remember... I don't know if you do, but I don't remember doing homework when I was in high school. But I remember Dick doing homework. He was a fairly serious student. He was somebody who, even at a young age, was sort of able to look at the world and have an opinion about it and not be.... have a pretty clear idea of what he thought how something should go. So, he was somebody you could go to and talk about with something and he would express an opinion. You know there are people in your life that you go to and you say, "Well, what do you think about this?" He was sort of one of those folks.

Wayne: Did he have an opinion about most things?

David: I think he probably.... if he was aware of them, I think he did. We were always very supportive of each other. My dad, when we were young, was a big guy....6-4, 200-something pounds ... even though we were getting larger we never got that big. Dad would roughhouse with us and sometimes when we were at the pool he would throw us in the pool, and something like that. So, we would sort of get organized and say, "OK," we won't let each other get to him at the pool.... would make a pact and it was sort of a way we would protect each other. And we teased Dorothy that she wasn't a member of this pact because she was a girl, but I guess we tried to protect her, too.

I remember when we would go down to the barn and feed the animals in the early '60s in junior high, early high school, we'd be going around the barn and we'd be singing the Four Seasons songs that were out just before the Beatles songs were out. We would sing those to each other. We would work on projects together. We would make kites, and the sled track that I talked to you about.

When I went to college Dick and I would call each other once a week. Now people call each other five times a day but back then it was expensive to make phone calls. He had to go find a phone booth and Dick would always start out those conversations by saying, "Hey, David. How's da broads?" And I'd say, "The broads is good." That was just a tag line (we used).

When I was a junior, Dick was a freshman in high school so we only had those two years together in high school. I think he was probably in (Student) Council one of those first two years at least.......

I think he was there in Council when Billy Moncrief was Council President my senior year (1967-68), I think Dickie was on there and he was on the track team with me. I was in the high jump and he was doing the pole vault. He used to love that: sort of running down and going up over the thing with the pole and that was the old days when we had solid aluminum poles, not the flexible ones they have today.

And we used to take guitar lessons together. Mom would always encourage us to be together, and when we didn't want to be together she would push us back together. So as far as the old garage bands and stuff that we had that was always largely Mom's push, that we stayed together, and that was nice that she did that.

Dick wasn't a great guitarist. He was good, but...I mean, he liked doing it...but I don't think it was his main interest.

Wayne: Randy (Motz) said that the group Rainn kind of broke up because he didn't think Dick liked performing in public.... that's the quote I got from him, that Dick was a good guitar player but he wasn't driven to perform in public like that, yet he played in the pit band for the musicals on guitar. I guess it was something about him not being the center of attention or focus onstage.

David: I don't know. I guess...I guess he was still like the little brother between Randy and I. You must have had that experience with your big brothers.... (Wayne's oldest brother Dick graduated HCHS class of 1966, and other brother Bob was HCHS class of 1968 along with David.)

Wayne: Oh, yeah...absolutely.

David: They were big personalities.

Wayne: They were a tough act to follow in high school for me.

David: But, I told you, in our senior year, we were in two parts of the Devil's Cabaret. It was when Bobby (Dilts) was doing the Johnny Carson thing (as the host of the Cabaret). So, we were on with Rainn and we did "Everyone calls her.... "Windy" by The Association. But then we did a banjo thing with Bobby Moncrief, Billy Moncrief, Dickie and I and we did "Mountain Dew" with banjoes....and Bobby was playing a tub bass, and it was more of a comedy kind of a thing.

   Dick played guitar and I played the banjo that we got at Rice's auction for ten cents. I found it in the junk pile and put it back together. I had a mandolin and a banjo...it wasn't great art but it was fun. Dressed up like hillbillies and singing....

   The guitar lessons were fun. Our guitar teacher was Larry Salemo and he used to teach in back of Nolde's (the only music store in Flemington in the 1960s) when it was next to the pizza place in the shopping center. So, Dick and I would go in there. We'd split an hour lesson. I'd do the first half hour, he'd do the second half hour. Sometimes Larry would teach us duets and stuff like that. But my hands were bigger. I had the advantage that I was growing faster so I was able to do things that Dick was not able to do. But Larry would break up....at one point he broke up Bach's *Bourree* into two parts and he gave one of us the top part and the other one the bottom part and we would play that together as a duet but I got tired of waiting for Dick so I learned both parts. (Laughs.)

Dick and I, when we were in Rainn, we started writing some songs. Dick wrote a song called *Mushroom Man* and it was sort of supposed to be a protest song where the mushroom had to do with atom bombs or something like that. Mushrooms (then) didn't have the connotations they might have had 15 years later. It went: "Here comes the Mushroom Man, handing mushrooms as he goes. He goes over the world.... over the seas and around the world, and over the red hills and over the green fields and blue fields and on..." It was one of those C to D kind of songs.

But sometimes we would play together on the guitar. Remember the beginning of *Bus Stop*? – bum bum, bum bum, bumbumbumbum.... and we would just play a riff off of that back and forth so it sounded kind of like baroque with each playing a different part.

So, he was a creative guy and enjoyed being creative.

Mom sort of instilled in us a sense that the world was not always the way people told you it was, and I think tried to get us to think independently about things. I remember in the Kennedy election, Dick was too young to have an opinion yet and I was only, in 1960, 10 years old. I came home wearing a Richard Nixon pin because he was the Vice President and I knew who he was. Mom said, "Why are you wearing that?" I said, "Because he is running for President." And Mom said, "Maybe we don't support Richard Nixon." Just talking the plus and minus, back and forth about things. But that kind of.... whatever people thought was red, she'd say, "Well, maybe it's blue." She was always able to point out both sides and I think Dick picked up a lot of that, too. Although having sampled both sides, he usually came down strongly on one side.

I think it was sort of a natural thing for him to sort of embrace the world that Nancy represented because the Quakerism, the drawing to service and all that, it pitted well within his view of himself and what he wanted to be.

Wayne: Did he ever do anything that surprised you?

David: Um…(Pauses.) …. yeah. He broke up with Jackie. (Laughs.) I think she's probably still conflicted. I think that she really loved Dick, she loved the family, things …. Life goes different ways…. People approaching their 60s must realize that children in their 20s are not necessarily fully responsible.

In high school, my science project was …. we took some frogs that we caught from the pond and then we…it's kind of gross…. we cut off the frogs' heads and took out the pituitary glands and then injected the pituitary glands into another frog and that induced ovulation in the frogs. So, the female frog gets a really big abdomen. What frogs do is, when they mate they sit up on top of each other like most animals but the male frog squeezes the abdomen to make the eggs come out and then sperm gets deposited over the eggs as they are coming out. Well, my female frog didn't have any guys around so we had to squeeze the abdomen for her and those eggs came out and you take a very thin glass needle … you just prick the edge of the eggs under the microscope with the glass needle … the eggs have to be coated with a little bit of frogs' blood, which we have around, then the eggs begin dividing, so we were following the growth of those frog embryos and stopped them here and there to show the different growths. Genetically, it's an interesting thing because they're clones of the mother because you activated growth in the … but it's actually only half the chromosomes. But they can grow to be full frogs. I didn't grow any out that far, so I've been telling people that I've been doing in vitro fertilization since I was 16. (Laughs.) Dick helped me with that. I was probably a senior or something.

Wayne: And then the two of you went to medical school together?

David: Yes. My life path was that I was a bio science major at Rutgers and I did not get into medical school first task. I went to graduate school and I got to live with my college roommate in Boston. He was in the Coast Guard because he got about a 10 or 11 in the draft lottery and I got 350 or something, so I went to graduate school and he went to the Coast Guard. (Chuckles.) He was two years ahead of me. We were in the first lottery altogether.

We lived in Quincy, Massachusetts, and I commuted into BU on the trains or rode my bike in. Dick would come up and visit us. We went to the St. Patrick's Day parade in South Boston one year. We always had interesting people visiting us there. There was a young lady from South Africa who's also English and Dick was there that same time and we were all standing there and the IRA float came by, and the young English lady from South Africa starting yelling, "Murderers!" and we all kind of turned around and said, "Who's that girl?" (Laughs.) But Boston was an interesting place to be and so when I got back, or when I was finishing up that program, Iris and I were engaged to be married. I decided I was going to go to medical school so I was going to go to Guadalajara if I didn't get in in the United States. Dick was applying at the same time because that was his natural time to apply. Dad had some teaching privileges at Rutgers at the time, and so Dick Mason, who was the Dean of Admissions and the Dean of Student Affairs later and he called up Dad...Iris and I were coming back from visiting Guadalajara, so we were at the airport....and he called up Dad and told him that both Dick and I had gotten into Rutgers. Dad called us at the airport, and Iris was happy that she didn't have to move to Mexico, and I was happy because I got to spend another two years with Dick.

So Dick was a "heads down" studier and he did very well. He was getting As all the time. I would get Cs. But it was nice to be together. It was really Pass/Fail....it didn't make any difference in terms of your transcript. But he was a hard worker.

Wayne: Did you live together?

David: No. He lived with Nancy and some other folks and I lived with Iris because we were married by then, and Iris ended up working for Dr. Mason as his secretary, so Iris sort of knew everybody at that school, too. And Dick and I played together, actually we had a sort of a Cabaret at medical school. Dick and I played together. We did *Will the Circle be Unbroken*. When we used to sing that together at home, we would change the verse where it says "they are carrying my mother" to "they are carrying my brother" so it wouldn't make my mother feel bad.

In the summer (of 1969), the guys that I would later room with that year ... we were going to a lot of festivals that year. We went to the Newport Folk Festival, we went to the Philadelphia Folk Festival. I guess Newport was early, the middle of July? Dick didn't go to those but Dick had the notion that he wanted to go to this Woodstock Festival. I think he actually got the tickets... no. We ended up buying the tickets on the way there. But it was Dick's idea and I said "Okay." My other friends were not up for going to that one, so Dick and I took off. I had an old blue Chevy II station wagon. It was what I had taken to college with me. It was one of Dad's old cars, and we drove up to Woodstock.

We started to look around and didn't see any festival anywhere and went to a supermarket and asked where the festival was and they said they had moved it over to White Lakes. I think they were selling tickets there in the supermarket or something and we bought two tickets and we got back on the Thruway and went all the way out to White Lakes. We got into town late on Friday night, I guess, whatever the first night was. It was 10 or 11 o'clock by the time we got in out of traffic and of course there was nowhere to stay but somehow or other but we ended up near a place called the Kensington Hotel, which was a boarded-up Catskills hotel, and it wasn't that well-boarded up because a bunch of folks had found their way into it. We went in there...we walked through one of the windows. There were some old creaky matresses and rather than sleeping in the car we slept on those matresses.

The next morning, we got up and started walking from the town of White Lakes towards the festival, towards the farm. Walking up there kind of reminded me of what it looked like with refugees because there were people walking this way and that, and back down the road and of course nobody's car is getting there because of all of the traffic jams that were there. In all that walking up and down the road I actually saw a young lady that I had seen in Newport about two or three weeks before. That was funny because among 50,000 people, you run into someone you know.

So we walked there and had our tickets in hand and there's no gate. Dick was looking around to see where we could hand the tickets in and it became clear that there wasn't anywhere to do so which is, I guess, the other reason why we still have them. We walked up on the hill and it was a little bit hot that day.

I don't remember the music that much. I mean there certainly were a lot of people smoking dope and doing acid. We were not. I mean I'd puff on a joint if it was passing by but we weren't doing anything more than that. I was smoking cigarettes at the time and I remember bumming cigarettes from somebody walking by. Of course, there wasn't any food. We were walking around and we saw that they were handing out corn. We ended up staying in this one spot which was three quarters of the way up the hill and a little off to the left of the stage. It looks big when you look at the pictures but it was just like any farm hill we have in Flemington.

We didn't have sleeping bags with us. I'm not sure what we envisioned what we were going to do but we were kind of sitting on the ground. Every now and then some spaced-out guy would go running by and somebody naked would go running by but we were mostly trying to listen to the music. They played all night, all the way until the morning. I think I fell alseep first. I think Dick heard The Who but I didn't hear the introduction of *Tommy* which was the first time they ever played that. I woke up when Sly and the Family Stone and Janis Joplin were singing.

It was mostly cold. We kind of huddled together there on the hill, kind of spooned. There were some other people there and we were all kind of spooning together just to be warm. Then it rained a bit. And finally, on Sunday morning, so we must have gotten through the whole weekend, we were kind of wet and cold and we decided not to stay until the end of the Festival. We walked down to the bottom of the hill and there was mud up to somewhere between my knees and my waist because all of the rain had kind of washed down the hill – probably the original mosh pit – and as we left, Gracie Slick was singing. I remember looking at her and thinking she looked a little tired and strung out herself. But we were about 15 feet from the stage when we walked out.

And that was Woodstock. And Dot never forgave us for not bringing her there. And I think Dick and I were happy to have shared the experience even though, in practice, it was cold and you couldn't hear the music that well, and there wasn't any food.

But Dick was very proud of having gone to Woodstock and I

remember when the movie came out which seemed like forever but was only a year or two later, he was really gung ho we should go see it. I think he was still with Jackie then. So we saw the movie and I think that was an important thing for him. It was important for me, too, but at this point it is more bragging rights – "I was there" – but I think it had more philosophical weight for him. I don't know. It seemed to move him more. And of course I appreciate it as a memory of him.

Then the next summer (1970), we went to California. Did I tell you about that? The merciful hot dog? I don't know if you knew the Kassels... They were friends. They lived on Mine Street next to Tommy Johnson. The Johnsons and the Kassels lived next door to each other, I think. They moved to California sometime while we were in high school. They were friends of my mom's. And Dick ...there had been some article in *Time* magazine about people driving up Highway 1, the Coast Highway, back then, so Dick and I decided we were going to drive up the Coast Highway. So Dick and Fred Huber and David Urbach and I rented one of these big trailer-like things that you drive in...

Wayne: Like a motor home?

David: Like a motor home. We left from the Los Angeles area and we drove all the way up the Coast Highway to Oregon. We stopped at Mendacino, California, and a commune on the way, so it was an interesting week. We put the camper on the beach and we got up in the morning ... it was deserted when we got there... and when we got up in the morning there were trucks all over the place... not trucks but little vehicles, and they were serving breakfast and they were filming a movie. There was this woman and she came out of the grocery store and she dropped her bags and the boy picked up the bags and handed them to her, and they they would do it over again. They did it about 30 times. They were filming *The Summer of '42*. Of course, we didn't know who any of those people were. But you never know when you see them filming a movie, but that's what they were doing.

Dick wasn't scared of climbing. He would scurry up these little cliffs with no problems. I was a little bit more fearful. The beautiful highways along the Pacific coast... we went up to San

Francisco, we camped out on the...we put the camper down by Fisherman's Wharf. I had a dream, but I can't remember now if it's a dream or if it's real that we hung out with The Grateful Dead then, but I'm pretty sure it was a dream. (Laughs.) But you know how your memory is.

And then we went all the way up to Mount Shasta in Oregon. We did go to one of these diners where they wouldn't let us in because it said "No hippies" on the door. Then we picked up these two girls on the road...we used to pick up everybody who was hitchhiking so we had like nine or ten people in the camper because it was a big place. You couldn't tell who was who. Nobody knew who the owner of the camper was, really. So we picked up these two girls, it was a girl and her girlfriend who was a former nun. And the girl's name was Mo.

We went all the way up somewhere in Washington and Mo dragged us to another house that she knew of that had been foreclosed, and we ended up camping....well, not camping out, staying in these people's living room . And I remember they made tuna casserole or something like that and Mo was running around the room naked ... she wasn't a beautiful girl but she was... different. And it was a lovely place with a view down to the water, and she told us that on the way back down we should stop by the Mirage Garage.

So we all went down the coast and we were looking for the Mirage Garage and we found a campfire and...remember, this is true...these two odd people sitting around the campfire and one of them only had two fingers like this, and they were making coffee... it was late in the evening... and we were talking about where everybody was from, and this fellow said he was raised by wolves and he had a friend Jeremiah who was a bullfrog and he went on with the words of that song but before we knew of that song... maybe they knew of it in California, I don't know. It was an odd coincidence.

We ended up going to a commune where we stayed for a couple of days. We went swimming in a lake that was a glacial stream and it was very, very cold.

So that was our California trip.

Wayne: This was the summer of 1970.

David: Yes, the summer of '70 after Dick had graduated from high school.

Appendix K

Interview with Dot Barad via telephone – January 26, 2014

Wayne: The Barad children, meaning your generation, seem to have been raised in a rather fearless way, and you've lived your lives that way and I was wondering if you could comment on that.

Dot: Well, I think some of that has to do with being... I'll use the word 'different.' My parents were college-educated, moved us out into the boonies in Delaware Township which was extremely rural and we were, with the exception of our next-door neighbors, we were the only two Jewish families in Delaware Township. So, I have to say I basically grew up identifying myself as being different from everyone else.

And there were moments in my life when I was rejected for being different, but I think I was pretty well prepared for that because I already understood who I was and if someone didn't like me for who I was, there wasn't much I could do to make it different.

Wayne: And that's the thread I see between you and David and also Dick ... I didn't know Bob as much ... that ... I want to call it 'thick-skinned" although I'm not sure I would use that expression ... does that come, do you think, from your mom and dad?

Dot: My mother (laughs) more than my father because there is the persona you show and the persona you don't show and in his personal life he does not have thick skin, but my mother does.

Wayne: Okay. What do you remember most about Dick?

Dot: Oh, his sense of humor. Actually, I sent a letter to Linda (a classmate of Dick's). Dick and Linda went to the Military Ball together (in 1968) and Linda was crowned Queen of the Military Ball and she had asked him to go with her, and she would say, "What a generous person he was because he accepted my invitation and I'm sure he had other options," etcetera, etcetera, and I'm thinking to myself, at that point in time he was actually very shy, socially shy. I mean, people may not have realized that but then I remember telling him that I felt the same way and he gave me ten reasons why he disagreed with me (laughs) and that was kind of our relationship. Yeah, his sense of humor. And he had really big hands. I know that sounds like an odd thing to say but...

Wayne: Well, it takes a lot of dexterity to play the guitar. Didn't he also play the French Horn?

Dot: Yes, he did. He was actually in the pit band for all the musicals.

Wayne: In *Camelot*, he is listed as playing the guitar but I thought I remembered him also playing the French Horn.

Dot: In the marching band. When I was a freshman, Mr. Krauss (the band director at HCHS) made sure I was a twirler because he wanted me to play the oboe. You know, he made those decisions for people. I was sitting next to Shelley Scammell because she and I were best buddies because we went through music school together and she played the oboe, too. She and I weren't marching. So, we were sitting on the hillside chatting and talking and I heard Mr. Krauss yell, "Barad and Scammell." Well, 'Barad and Scammell' were always Dick and Charlie, never Shelley and I so we continued talking, and he kept yelling "Barad and Scammell. Barad and Scammell!" So finally, we looked up and everybody was looking at us and we were like, "Oh, my God. WE'RE 'Barad and Scammell'!" He wasn't clear. (laughs).

Wayne: Is there anything else you can think of that you would like me to address, or focus on, or emphasize?

Dot: I have said to you that one of his biggest concerns was being forgotten. He realized he was terminal and that he would die early, but over the years I have had many people tell me how they carry him both in their heads and in their hearts. I'm talking about people who haven't seen him in 40, 45 years... I mean, one person can have an impact on others and it doesn't.... the length of one's life, it doesn't matter on some levels because of that impact that keeps their spirit alive. You know as far as I am concerned, I would have wanted more... that's the bottom line, you know?

Wayne: Almost everyone I have talked to in the course of this project feels the same way. That those of you who were closest to him felt cheated in that he...

Dot: Not so much cheated when he passed. Obviously when he passed there was this incredible loss, and I always described it as... you know, when you're watching a really good movie or reading a really good book and then they wipe out one of the best characters in the first two chapters. You know? That hardly seems like a good story, right? Well, that's kind of like.... When it happened, he was such an accomplished character and he was such a well-adjusted person and he did a lot of the things he set out to do.

    At a time when I didn't have any goals, he told me that he had just moved the 5 – 10-year plan to the 2 – 3-year plan. And I looked at him and said, "You have a 5 – 10-year plan??" But as I am getting older and turning 60 in a couple of weeks...

Wayne: Welcome to the Club!

Dot: Thank you. (laughs) It's a good club, actually.

    It makes me have a longer perspective of all the things he missed having to do. As the years go by it becomes even harder. I think the hardest thing so far was Leah's wedding which I felt like I was living out a scene from *Carousel* since I have to think of everything in musical metaphors. But they were so inclusive of his memory and it was incredibly touching. At one point I was sitting at the table and my son Noah was on the other side of the table.... I was a little too far away. I could see him and he could see me and in the middle of the dinner when they were doing all the tributes and things like that, my phone started to buzz and I looked down and my son had sent me a text message. It said, "I wish I could walk over to you and give you a hug." And I was thinking, "Oh, my! It must be written all over my face." (laughs) I'm trying not to feel that way but you can't not feel that way.

Wayne: One of the things I've learned while digging into this Barad barrage of family information is how intensely devoted you are to each other even though you are often separated by continents. It is just a remarkable part of the story to me... that you all love so deeply and so dearly when you are with each other.

Dot: I think the hardest thing was ... the relationships were: "the boys" – David and Dick, then me and Bob. When I was referring to "my brothers," I wasn't referring to Bob, I was referring to David and Dick. And when David went off to college, he didn't really come home. He stayed away. So, that's how Fred Huber ended up in the clan because Fred would come home and he used to come over for dinner all the time and he kept coming over for dinner when David wasn't around. And then Dick and Fred and I started hanging out together and doing stuff because Fred had a car and Dick and I didn't. So, in the summer we would go to the movies and this and that. And then Fred and Dick became very, very close friends and David and Fred no longer had that much to do with each other. And then when Dick passed, I got to inherit Fred, which wasn't bad actually because I always liked Fred.

Wayne: And, by the way, I have never heard from him...

Dot: Well, he is one you should talk to...

Wayne: Well, if you would rattle that cage for me....

Dot: I will do that. I will have him call you. I will tell him that this is his last opportunity to get involved here, and Dick would not appreciate it if he didn't. The way the family relates to each other really has to do with the characters sitting around the table and you haven't had the experience of losing a sibling. There is the way you interact with (your brother) Bob and there is the way you interact with (your brother) Dick, and in terms of our situation, "the boys" were a unit and Dick and I were middle kids and Bob's the baby. And when Dick was gone, we all had to learn how to interact with this big hole in the middle. Not only was I the only girl, but now I was the only middle child, too, and it was hard.

Appendix L

Brother Bob remembers Dick:

Dick was, is, and will forever be one of the smartest guys I've ever known. Dick's kind of smart is both book-smart and people-smart. The Yiddish word that captures this best is *seychel*, meaning "good sense."

I resist thinking of him as gone from my life. I think that is because I continue to feel his powerful living example; his memory stays with me as a persistent call to make the most of every day with joy and purpose. Like Dick always did.

As the youngest in my family by a margin of more than five years, my elder siblings Dot, Dick, and David were all giants to me. But I noticed early on that some giants were bigger than others. A story at the fringes of my memory relates that I called both of my older brothers "Guy," differentiating them by height: "Big Guy" and "Little Guy." At some interval, I learned Dick's family nickname, so my nine-year-older brother David became "Big Dickie" and my seven-year-older brother Richard became known as... well, let's just say he was grateful when I grew out of that phase.

Dick's kind of people-smart extends beyond his Jedi skill of bringing caring friends and amazing women to share his inner circle. He was also a master at balancing justice and proportion.

He never feared to be different (we were all raised with this fearlessness), but Dick was no "rebel without a cause." Whether it was a student protest, campaigning for the right of 18-year-olds to vote, or providing family-centered medical care to his community,

Dick always selected his purpose with thoughtfulness and care. When the times demanded good people to work for rights and fairness, he would be present to answer the call, or to lead whenever the movement and the moment required it. He inspired.

Dick's kind of joy appreciates irony, even (or perhaps especially) when linked with adversity. During a summer break from college, Dick and his high school sweetheart Jackie took a trans-Europe road trip in a beat-up car. Near the far end of that journey, they accidentally sent their rooftop-placed travel documents flying to the wind as they pulled out of a petrol station in Tito's Yugoslavia. Dick retold the epic story of their slow return to the UK – carrying only a police report written in Serbo-Croatian to explain their misadventure – with expressions of accomplishment and delight that were uniquely his own.

When I went through difficult times in my early twenties, Dick offered a strong hand to reach out to for steady support. A premature end to my U. S. Peace Corps service had taken away our chance to be in Sierra Leone together during the year that Dick and his wife Nancy spent as volunteers in a rural community hospital, but all three of us learned a deep appreciation for the rich culture of West Africa. When I returned to Africa not long after Dick's death, Nancy traveled to our temporary base in Togo. Those days marked the completion of my mourning for a disrupted past and my first steps forward as a husband and future father.

Nancy and Dick's wedding offered up a lively mix of Jewish and Quaker family and traditions. It was the 1970s, and Nancy kept her family name, which by then was also her professional name. Marriage didn't change them. Both before and after, they remained doctors of family medicine: Dr. Barad and Dr. Scattergood.

Nancy once told me that when she lived with Dick before marriage, half of the people thought they were married. After marriage, half of the people thought they were living together. She noted it as an observation, not a complaint. Following convention was never the priority for either of them: living every day with joy and purpose was the goal. And that is an enduring gift they have passed on to their daughter Leah.

Leah Barad: the most purposefully conceived child of our family. When Dick and Nancy made the choice to start a family, they did so with the full medical knowledge that his brain cancer spelled distant odds for long-term survival. But they reached for parenthood anyway, and the world is so much luckier for that choice.

While it is the purpose of youth to reach for the sky, Dick's brain cancer brought all of us down to earth. Nobody lives forever, but we each have a role in ensuring that the human legacy of a loving spirit endures from one generation to the next.

Whenever a person dies young, they stay young in our memories forever. There are too many famous examples from our parents' generation of imperfect people transformed into stylized icons: Marilyn Monroe, Che Guevara, Martin Luther King, Jr., John and Robert Kennedy. We are tempted to paint them better than real life, but Dick's kind of Jedi knight does not aim for fame or perfection. We remember him as he would want to be remembered: a realistic radical, a caring friend and a loving family man, but more than anything, a guy with good sense.

I love my brother Dick. I miss him, but I will never lose him.

Bob Barad
World Food Programme
Dakar, Senegal
10 October 2013

Appendix M

A postscript about Bob Barad, as seen through Dot's eyes:

Ahhhh Bobby....

Bob was born while we still lived in Ringoes NJ. I remember we had a family meeting to name the new baby... I wanted it to be a girl so I could even up the score... two boys and two girls... but it was not meant to be. I remember I liked the name Alan and it was used as his middle name.

I do not remember much about Mom's pregnancy... but I do remember her leaving to go to the hospital. Bob is the only one of us born at the Hunterdon Medical Center.

His birthday is in April and I remember Dad taking us to the medical center with our telescope. Mom held the baby up to the hospital window and the three of us got our first look at Bobby though our telescope Dad set up in front of the hospital. Children were not allowed in the maternity ward, even if it was my Dad's maternity ward.

Bobby (is and) was a very inquisitive child, and once he started talking he never stopped asking questions. I think it was very hard being five years younger than I was and seven years younger than Dick and nine years younger than David.

I was the one had the most interaction with him as he was too little to join most things, so I always would say I have two brothers and Bob, meaning the boys were always seen as a unit of one... David and Dick....and Bob separately.

Dick really missed David when he left for college (and never did come home that much). As I have written before, Fred Huber came around a lot and they bonded very strongly in the absence of David.

When Dick left for college, I spent most of the last two years of high school figuring out how to get to Cornell as often as possible.

At this point, Bob was going to Buckingham Friends school as he was just too fast a learner to stay at Delaware Township school - they already skipped him one grade. But his older siblings were really involved in their own lives... Dick with his school work and Jackie in England.

I do have a letter from Dick telling me to be nicer to Bob and let Bob be a kid and what a really cool little guy he was (See Appendix N). How frustrating it must be for him to have only adults around him... I need to be more patient.

Dick wrote this to me during a school break where he overheard me frustrated with my little brother and decided to tell me how he felt. He wrote the letter but didn't give it to me; he waited until he returned to Cornell and sent it to me in the mail. I kept it, which means to me I found it important. I am a bit embarrassed by what he had to say but considering my age and the time, he was doing his best to help me steer my "boat" in a better direction.

To my relief, Bob and I are very close and he remembers only that I was a good kind sister. Bob was also very near sighted which we did not find out until he was in kindergarten and the school suggested we get his eyesight tested. When he got his glasses for the first time, he was amazed that people on television had faces and trees had leaves.

My parents took Bob to Kenya during Dick's senior year in high school, 1970. Dick and I were left home alone for two weeks or more. We had to cook and clean up (I voted for eating over the sink so we would have no dishes but Dick didn't like that idea). We were both involved in the school musical (along with you and Alan Goodman), *Camelot*. Dick was in the pit band and I was in the chorus. We were so busy with rehearsals that when my parents were about to return, Dick and I looked at each other in horror and realized we didn't even have one party while they were gone how embarrassing.

When I think back on how happy each of us were to finally be out of our parent' house and launched into the world, it makes me a little sad when I think about Bob being left behind going through high school with none of his siblings living nearby.

We were very loyal to each other and would always return home for the holidays… to see our parents but mostly to see each other knowing we would all be home. New Years was always fun. My parents always stayed in for New Year's Eve and my Dad always made a big spread of food and if we were very lucky it would snow and David and Dick with a crew of pals from the neighborhood would build these wonderful sled paths.

We were young, beautiful, and godlike … nothing bad would ever touch us … until it did.

Appendix N

On a visit home from Cornell during his first year in college in April, 1971, Dick overheard Dot complaining to one of her friends about Bobby's behavior. Dick wrote her the following letter that night and mailed it to her when he got back to college.

Dear Dot,

    I'm writing this Friday night, April 2. You're in the next room telling Barbara what a bad kid Bobby (you know the little kid) is. Well, you're wrong. And I would like to tell you right now but you wouldn't listen and you'd say I'm just taking his side and you'd tell me to get out and to stop listening, etc. So I'll write it, put it in the mail, and you'll read it. Pretty good idea, don't you think?

    Bobby is a kid. A kid is a kid. He's not a little adult. Kids do kids things and there is no reason why they shouldn't. I'd like doing kid things myself but you see – I'm an "adult," ha – like you – it's not allowed anymore. Kids have got to do kids things cause they're kids. If you don't let a kid be a kid – it fucks him up. Bobby's a kid. Kids are cool.

    Bobby isn't a regular kid. He's got a rather strange head. Did you ever read some of that poetry? Well, he's not a regular kid because he's a little kid in a big family. No friends. That's really poor. When I was a kid (or boy) well there were always friends. Moncriefs, Tray Bond, Bennet, Gary – it's hard to imagine no friends. Well the result is that in many ways Bobby is a little adult when he should be a kid. Like he thinks he can say intelligent things in "adult" conversations and he even thinks he's about equal with his sister who is <u>so</u> much older than he is. Not all the time but sometimes he gets that in his head. Well it's our fault. We tell him to grow up, don't be a baby, don't be silly, etc. So, he's a kid who wants to be like the big kids because he sees that as the way to get respect in this house.

    He also sees it as the only way to have any fun in life because he doesn't really know how far out it is just to be a kid.

    So first, if you feel challenged by him – that's your own fuck up. You're you and he's him (rotten English) and there is no reason why you should worry about your relative status if you have a good idea of who you are. Chances are that when he starts growing he's going to be bigger than you or I and you may have to get used to being the little sister... again. But you really should realize that it doesn't begin to make a bit of difference. If he bugs you – if you are not so secure about the whole thing – well ignore him but don't put him down and don't let it wreck a whole night.

I sound like some sort of fucking ridiculous older brother, don't I? Well of course I am not like that so take the whole thing with salt.

Well just remember kids are kids and why not? Bobby's a kid. Get him to write more cause he might be good. Every time you tell him to do or not do something try and think if there is any <u>real</u> reason he should do what you say. I mean a real reason. Don't try to show who's boss cause that is silly – you know who's boss and besides – what's the dif? Let him be a kid as much as he can cause he's never been a kid enough. If he's wrong don't tell him how bad he is – tell him what he did wrong, he'll know how bad he is.

I don't really know what I am talking about of course but these thought(s) pop into my head so why not write them down? Well just think about it – it seems pretty simple. If you think I'm all wrong tell me to get fucked.

Love, Dick

P.S. As of this moment, I'm not going to say (or write) "<u>fuck</u>" anymore!

Appendix O

Jackie's emails to Wayne

Jackie Herbert still lives in England. In response to my request for her memories of "life with Dick Barad," she sent me a series of the following three emails.

December 2, 2011

OUT OF THE BLUE

The beginning of my story of meeting Dick started a year earlier in the summer 1968. I was a skinny girl with long brown hair and a short skirt and I was checking out the notice board at the sixth form College where I was studying English Literature, and History of Art 'A Level' in my hometown of Sutton Coldfield in England. I was 17 and I hadn't got a clue what direction to take my life. At least, all the big decisions about college and career loomed and I was hesitating. I couldn't imagine how Art or English Lit. both of which I loved, could actually earn me an eventual living, so I was stuck.

Basically, I was procrastinating. But sometimes life, especially when we are not expecting it, comes up trumps and hands us something special as though it had just been waiting for us to ask. And there, on the notice board, was an invitation for students to apply for a year's study programme in the US. A gift. Out of the blue.

I jumped at the chance.

The programme was AFS, American Field Service, an international exchange programme originally set up by British and American ambulance crews during the 1st and 2nd world wars. Friendships, which had been made on the battlefields, which had survived and flourished during peacetime, eventually becoming a blueprint for an inspired initiative to forge bonds between nations through simple friendship.

The idea was aimed at young people (theoretically the future decision makers) to give an experience of living in a different country for a year, hopefully encouraging understanding and lasting links. It was hoped that the friendships created would promote peace and consequently the possibility of conflict between countries would be less likely.

It was a good programme, efficiently set up, and careful to match student with appropriate hosts. But first the hurdles. AFS only took A or B grade students, the weeding out process was intense, and the interviews stiff. AFS didn't just want good students, they wanted ambassadors. All this went on for months until, in late the spring of 1969, I received a longed-for letter of acceptance. I remember clearly that my face was literally stuck in an enormous and ridiculous grin for days afterwards. I must have looked insane! These days, to travel is completely normal for young people, but in those days I might just as well have set off for the moon! My parents were encouraging about the trip, they came with me to the endless interviews and were happy for me when I heard that I had achieved a place on the 1969/70 AFS scholarship programme. I was ecstatic, I couldn't stop smiling for days.

By August I was flying into the US with 50 other British students when the flight captain spoke over the loudspeaker and explained that there was a large festival happening below at a place called Woodstock. Welcome to America.

MEETING THE MOTZES

My first days in America were an onslaught of impressions and experiences. The intense heat and smell of summer greeted us on arrival at JFK, then we drove on to spend some days at Hofstra University on Long Island waiting for our adoptive families. Many students flew on to other States, my family, the Motzes, came and fetched me.

We had written and exchanged photographs for weeks beforehand. Now I met Ralph and Dot, my new 'parents' in person. Ralph was dark haired and strong-looking, he wore a checked shirt and had a good hand shake. He was a skilled cabinetmaker and carpenter. His wife, Dot, was a petite blonde with a great smile and a generous manner. The kids were, Randy, a little older than me and at home from University for the summer, he had a shock of pale brown hair, and a big grin behind the moustache. Pam, friendly but a little reserved, was about my age, an attractive girl with dark, shoulder length hair. Brian was the youngest, about 11 at the time, I think, smiling, with pale hair and wearing glasses.

The family were welcoming and full of chatter as we set off on a very scary ride home via the New Jersey Turnpike, I had never seen such a vast road system before, nor such big cars or huge lorries. Ralph drove with one hand holding his beer, with the window rolled right down and the other hand loosely holding the steering wheel. At one point, we took the wrong exit then reversed back, I wondered if we would make it home in one piece.

After the Turnpike, the countryside became softer, rolling farmland. It looked a lot like some of the southern counties of England but seemed more lush and scented, with the sound of crickets in the midsummer heat. Whenever I have returned over the years, the scent of the air is so reminiscent of that time.

We drove through the town of Flemington. I thought it was wonderful, rather old-fashioned and looking like photos I had seen. I liked the style of the houses, rather Scandinavian with porches and open space around. Later I learned it had a real sense of community, which I found attractive.

We drove on to the Motzes house. It was a classic wooden house set into the countryside, surrounded by farmland. It had a deep porch and good proportions and a good-sized garden with trees. I loved it from the beginning

The inside of the house was a kind of colonial style, with white curtains and linen. Dot kept the place beautifully and I later learned was a great home-maker. My room was downstairs and I was surprised by two things, starting with a rack of real guns hanging on the wall. I had never seen a gun before arriving in America until I saw the police who were obviously armed, but still, a wall of guns seemed very surprising. Then, the following morning the sound of children's TV. In England in those days, television didn't come on until the afternoon or evening, so TV early in the morning seemed amazing. I discovered Brian sitting cross-legged eating cereal and watching cartoons. Bliss for boys.

It was the next day that Dot had arranged for us all to visit friends called the Barads for something called Brunch. As it turned out, I liked both things a lot.

June 22, 2012

I find it hard to find my way back, I have been avoiding it. It was a different life, almost someone else's.

I suppose for us all, for Dick's friends and family, our memories are a Kaleidoscope of impressions, half remembered conversations, events, feelings, emphasis.

So it was, particularly on the second morning of my arrival in Flemington, as the Motzes and I went to brunch with the Barads. Within the house, which in itself was extraordinary to me, so modern, so much space, the atmosphere was friendly, expansive, and slightly chaotic, with people coming and going, flurries of impressions, conversation and snatches of music. It left me with a lasting affection for The Barad family.

I remember that the family seemed so outgoing and confident, I was at that time pretty shy and spent a lot of time pretending not to be, so the onslaught of so many, it felt like 'so many', confident people in one place was something to get used to. I was introduced to Bea, who welcomed me warmly and who was in the process of cooking vast amounts of French toast and bacon, all served up with syrup and fruit. Bea is an amazing woman and I was charmed from the first. Later I met Gerry and saw how they fitted together, and what a team they made. When Gerry came home from work he would grab whichever of his kids was passing at the time and they would disappear into a great bear hug of affection. It was attractive to see a family who seemed so at ease.

I met Dot who was simply beautiful. With her big smile, clouds of hair and willowy figure she was lovely, a year younger than me and still a girl really, I liked her straight away. She has been a friend to me over the years and supportive when sometimes life has been difficult.

I met David who was at college and later his girlfriend, Iris, who was to become his wife. They looked happy and good together. Because David was at college he seemed very grown up, a couple of years seemed like a lot then and I was shy.

Bob, on the other hand, was only about eleven when I first met him. A boy with a mop of dark hair and big spectacles, he was at the mercy of his sibling's endless teasing and frustrated at not being old enough to be included in everything that David, Dick,

Dot and their friends were up to. Later that summer I remember the older boys threw Bob into the old pool and he emerged soaking and screaming that he had been poisoned by all the bugs and bacteria he had swallowed ... he was very scientific even then.

Years later Bob turned up in London, where I was living at the time, and I saw that little Bobbie had grown up and was a tall young adult and had finally caught up with us all. Even later he generously invited me to his son Richard's bar mitzvah in Rome which was a joyous celebration of family and friends. The presence of Dick during those few days was almost tangible, there are echoes of him in both his nephews, a smile or a walk, I saw it in Leah too when she came to London a few years later, older then than when I first met Dick. Meanwhile, the days in Rome were a chance for us all to talk, to remember, to include.

So, back to brunch in the summer of 1969 where I met Dick for the first time. There was so much going on that morning and so much to take in, but Dick was a naturally memorable person. I suppose my first impression was of a good-looking boy with a great smile and an easy manner dressed in blue jeans and an open neck shirt. He was taller than me and had a mass of dark curly hair brushed into submission from a side parting. The most striking feature from the beginning, though, were his eyes which seemed to literally sparkle. Dick's eyes were always full of life whatever he was doing, they just pulled you in.

That morning was full of joking and talking, as were many other times to follow, the siblings teasing, the Motzes joining in, the atmosphere easy, talking about everything from music to politics. I came to love the two families, and later went on to enjoy friendships with many of the new people I met in Flemington. But I was attracted to Dick. Even that first day I saw what fun he was to be with, he would crease up with laughter, jostle with his friends and family and fool about. From the beginning I learned, too, that Dick and his friends were not just lightweights, they took political issues seriously, they cared about social justice, environmental change, and the possibility of change. I admired the commitment shown by my new friends and especially admired Dick and his ambition to make a difference and do his best in the world. I had never been exposed to that kind of awareness before in my own peer group at home, so this was really interesting to me.

1969 - 70 was a time of great change. The Vietnam war showed no sign of letting up and as students we watched, appalled, as our peers were issued with numbers from the draft board. At Kent State University, a group of protesting students were shot and killed by troupers; a sweating Nixon appeared on television to 'explain' the US presence in Cambodia. Candle lit peace marches filed across the country, young men came home maimed from a war that they didn't believe in. Meanwhile, men had walked on the moon and we students at Hunterdon Central were given photographs from Kodak of the historic landing. The year was punctuated by peace marches and music festivals, hippies danced.

For me that year, at the edge of two decades, remains full of vivid and varied memories, but ultimately Dick was at the centre. He was committed to his work, the school and his grades. He was aiming for Cornell and needed to focus, he was president of the school council and needed to be involved in that, he played in the marching band and needed to give time to that. While I admired it all it nearly drove me mad that he seemed to have no time for anything else, especially not a girlfriend!

By the autumn of '69 I was being asked out to the Military Ball and was turning down potential escorts in the vain hope that Dick would ask me. At that point he also had managed to break his arm so I wasn't even sure if he would show up! As the song says 'it's no fun being a teenager in love'. But, Dick f i n a l l y did ask me to the Ball and we had a great time. Unfortunately, on the way home the car stopped dead and we realized that he had forgotten to fill the car with petrol so that we ended up having to walk half a mile back to his house in deep snow, me wearing an evening dress. Dick was embarrassed but we pretty soon saw the funny side and I was perfectly ok so laughing and shivering we trudged our way back home. Bea was waiting and gave him a very hard time for making me walk in snow on such a cold night!

As the year went on Dick was still infuriatingly disciplined about studying and work but we met up at school and spent time together during holidays and some weekends. He was driven and worked hard, I admired his focus. For me the school year at Hunterdon Central was very different from home and I was enjoying everything. Also, the AFS scheme that I was on provided weekends hosted by different towns to get together with other scholarship students who were within a distance of 100 miles or so. The monthly weekend gatherings were a blast and I met so many extraordinary students from a dozen or more countries who remained friends for years afterwards. At the end of the summer term we all left our host families and traveled together for two weeks before getting on our respective planes and heading home.

It suddenly struck both Dick and I that my departure was imminent. For me it was terrible, to leave, and he too was feeling pretty rotten about it. We didn't know if we would see each other again. We did have a chance to meet before I got onto the plane home but then I had to go. The song *Leaving on A Jet Plane* rang in our ears.

In my absence I had been accepted onto a Foundation Art course in my local home town in England. They allowed me to fast track 2 years into 1 then to apply for Art School and a degree from there. It was intense but I remember missing Dick very much. He, by then, had been accepted by Cornell to study medicine. We wrote long letters which was the only way to keep connected in those days and not a compensation for being apart.

Over the following four years our relationship was trans-Atlantic, consisting of long letters, some rare phone calls (the cost was so high), and visits back and forth, always during the Christmas or summer holidays, Dick would fly to Europe, I would go to the US. It was inevitably difficult but in some ways it was good for us both as we were able to concentrate on our work. I loved to visit Dick and was interested in the life he led at Cornell.

When I went up there the life on campus was new to me, the buildings, what people talked about, the way they behaved and dressed, the music, the sweltering summer heat, stories of the deep winter snow. Some things were familiar, the slum landlords, student parties with loud music and bad wine, junk food, the perennial balancing act between a big workload and a social life, the desire to succeed.

At home my Foundation course led to a place at Kingston College, London, which in those days was one of the three leading Design colleges in England. I was amazed to get in, the competition was tough and the reputation of the course very high. England was buzzing at that time as a centre for Design, Fashion and Music. It was a good moment to be following this kind of career. The college was run by the legendary Daphne Brooker and the pressure never let up. The curriculum was intense and challenging. Projects were run by visiting lecturers from industry and fashion and we all wanted to impress, there was never enough time, the criticism was vicious, and the atmosphere wholly competitive. Welcome to the world of Fashion.

Despite it all I thrived. I could do it. I loved the work, I won competitions, I got my designs photographed and included in Vogue magazine, I was part of a team to represent England in Europe, (and) I won a travel bursary from the Royal College of Arts. I liked my fellow students, I worked hard. I had a great job at the end of it all.

While I was a student I was sharing an apartment with four other friends at the top of a big Victorian pile. It was spacious but owned by a slum landlord and in the winter was freezing. Dick came over one winter from the subzero temperatures and deep snow of Cornell and said he had never been so cold in his life! It's the damp of course, we were all so cold. I spent as much time as I could in the evenings working in the college studios which had heating, or sometimes in desperation in the local laundramat. I hate being cold.

Then in the summer break, I would have the chance to go back to Flemington to see Dick. It was so good to get together again. Those summers were very special.

July 13, 2012

It was always wonderful to fly into JFK airport to meet up with Dick again. It did take time for us to get used to each other again after months apart but the summertime was special catching up with what Dick had been doing, meeting up with friends, catching up with all the new things happening. Sitting in the pool to cool off, the dogs tearing down the hill, two mountain Pyrenees and one toy poodle (who thought she was a mountain Pyrenees), helping to bottle tomatoes from Gerry and Bea's huge harvest, going to Rice's market, visiting Martha's Vineyard.

I remember flying down to Lynchburg, Virginia, one summer for a visit to see my host family, the Motzes, who had moved there earlier. It was so nice to see them and I stayed for a few days but coming back to Flemington I remember walking into the Barad house to a completely rapturous greeting from Dick who ran through the house shouting "Jackie's back! Jackie's back!" Part of Dick's great charm was his ability to switch from 'serious young man' to crazy and lighthearted in a blink, it was endearing.

What was slightly less endearing was his stubbornness. I myself am horribly stubborn too, so I could easily recognize the quality and it led to situations like the incident below.

One summer we went up to Canada on a road trip. We borrowed Bea's little blue car and set off using a very small tent. We had never got around to buying a hammer for the tent so this meant we always struggled to bash in the tent pegs to concrete-hard ground with any rock we could find.

One evening we arrived late at a campsite in Montreal which was on the banks of the St Lawrence River. The ground was very hard, all the best spots had been taken and we ended up erecting the tent in what turned out to be a Very Bad Place despite warnings from other campers. Dick was determined that it would be fine no matter what. When the rain came in the night we were woken by streams of water flowing around and through the little tent and were obliged to rescue the collapsing thing and move it to higher ground as the stream we had pitched in coursed down the hill. Dick did his best to cheer us both up as we struggled with the tent and the storm.

Sometime later during the night I woke to a mosquito buzzing. I was so tired that I just turned over and went back to sleep. When I opened my eyes again the 18" above my head was black with hundreds of the noisy and hungry insects sheltering from the storm with us. I learned that camping wasn't really my favorite thing.

THE GRAND TOUR

Despite my reservations about camping, and because we were poor students with no money, when Dick and I decided we would like to spend some time touring through Europe we set off again (summer 1971) in a borrowed car (my mother's) filled with provisions and carrying a tent!

It was an epic trip in lots of ways. The car we had borrowed was my mother's ancient yellow Triumph Herald cheerfully referred to as the 'Yellow Peril' loaned with warnings from my father about something called The Big End, whatever that was. .

The trip began cheerfully in France but became slightly stressful in Paris as we lost the Boulevard Peripherique and ended up with Dick determinedly crunching gears around the insanity of the road system which circles the Arch De Triomphe. Having survived that, our trip continued across France where we were nearly arrested by the side of a mountainous road for trying to break into our own car with a wire coat hanger (don't ask!) after locking the keys inside, an easy mistake to make.

Halfway across Italy The Peril started making appalling noises as we drove at 70 mph down the autostrada. We discovered that if we went faster it didn't sound so bad.

Despite this temporary and dangerous solution, we were eventually forced to pull into a service station to find help. This resulted in my getting out of the car to let the engineer climb in, which resulted in Dick driving off down the motorway WITHOUT ME, which resulted in me being left alone at a service station somewhere in Italy, with no ID, no money, no telephone, and wearing only a tee shirt and a pair of shorts! Not an ideal situation.

Dick had thought he was just being directed to the service area. In fact, the service was actually on the OTHER side of the motorway which resulted in him finding himself, to his horror, driving back into the motorway traffic accompanied by an engineer who didn't speak English, having left his girlfriend behind.

Hours later I spotted Dick again, frantically waving to me from the other side of 6 lanes of fast moving traffic after he had left the motorway, paid the toll, rejoined the motorway and finally retraced his route to end up on the 'service' side. I was extremely relieved to see him.

The problem with the car, once it had been hoisted onto a ramp, was identified as a tear on the inside of a tire, banging against the wheel arch. We had been incredibly lucky that it hadn't burst as we drove at speed. The engineer was baffled when Dick and I looked hugely happy ... we were just glad it wasn't the mysterious Big End whatever that was.

We chugged on towards Yugoslavia where we promptly lost all our important documents on the first evening. Dick had placed the wallet containing our money, passports, return ferry tickets, and all other travel documents on the roof of our car after filling the car with petrol. Then we drove off.

Trying to travel in a Communist country without ID or travel documents isn't a good plan. We ended up the next morning face to face with a very large policewoman straight from Central Casting who sat underneath a photograph of General Tito and did not look happy. In the end, we got off lightly and were sent across country to Zagreb where there was both an American and British embassy to get replacement ID. Zagreb was a friendly place and Dick and I both really liked the Yugoslavian people. It was appalling to think of what happened to that country only a few years later.

We drove back across Europe using our new ID, two sheets of paper written in Serbo-Croatian which no one could understand but did have our photographs attached, amazingly the borders let us in. In those days, it was impossible to travel across a border without a Green Card Insurance document, how we managed to do it I can't imagine. I think thanks to Dick's American Express card which he somehow still had, we had enough cash to survive.

We made our way back across southern Europe, it was chaotic and fun, and by the time we made it to the south of France the old car was just about still going, although by then the silencer had dropped off so the noise we made when going through towns and villages was quite impressive. Also, by now the car didn't really take to climbing mountains very well so that we had to stop every fifteen minutes to take off the radiator cap to release the steam to let her cool down. It took us ages to get over the Pyrenees.

Getting back across the English Channel was complicated by an international money crisis which made releasing money to pay for new ferry tickets a near thing. I hadn't been in contact with my family since Yugoslavia as I didn't want them to worry about the lack of documents. What Dick and I didn't know was that our papers had all been sent back to my home by an Austrian tourist who had found them on the floor of the Yugoslavian petrol station. Naturally, my mother got hold of these and couldn't imagine how we could manage without them...visions of Dick and I in a

Yugoslavian goal (jail)!

So, along with dozens of other cars, Dick and I drove off the ferry and, randomly, up to one of several immigration booths to present our documents. In our case this meant two scruffy pieces of paper written in Serbo-Croatian with our photos on. A surprising thing happened. The immigration officer examined our papers, looked at us carefully, then broke into a large smile and said,

"Oh, you're Dick and Jackie! I spoke to your mother this morning. She has phoned every port on the South coast of England begging us to let you in. Apparently, she has your passports!"

It was nothing short of humbling really.

Throughout the college years we wrote and met up when we could. But these were formative years and eventually the gaps between the letters became longer and longer (and) it became more and more obvious that not only the career paths we had individually chosen were quite different, but also our life experiences. Dick was focused on medicine; it was important and in comparison I felt pretty lightweight despite all the work I was putting in. In the end, it was my actions which caused our break up after five years. I am not proud of that but I am so grateful for the time we did have together which was so special. I have always been so grateful for those extraordinary years with Dick.

What was wonderful was that Dick and Nancy got together and were later married. They were so suited to each other and complimented each other well. I was lucky enough to see it when, years later, they stopped to visit on their way back from Africa in the summer of 1982. I was married to James and we had our first child, David. Dick and Nancy turned up in London on the day before we were moving home, everything was in packing boxes. It was a lovely surprise to see them and after doing some sightseeing in London, they joined us a few days later at our new home which was in a village in the Chilterns, 40 miles west of London. It was a really good couple of days, they even heroically picked up paintbrushes and helped us with painting our 'new', 200-year-old house. We had a chance to spend time with Dick and Nancy, to hear what they had been doing in Africa and what their plans for the future were. It was a very happy visit.

I didn't know it would be the last time I would ever see Dick.

Out of the blue one perfectly normal day, I was at home and received a phone call from Dick's family to explain that he was seriously ill and would like to talk for a while. It is a call I will always remember, it was shocking.

When I heard Dick speak I realized that he was saying "Goodbye." And that seemed impossible because Dick was so young and strong and determined and alive and he had a great life ahead of him with friends and family and work. This wasn't supposed to happen to healthy young people, Dick was much, much too young. It was the reaction we all must have had.

But mostly all I could think about was Nancy and their baby Leah. It was just so unfair.

I can't imagine how hard Dick's death has been on all his family. The thing that sticks with me is that Dick didn't have enough time with his family and he didn't have the chance to see Leah grow up and that seems very sad indeed.

A few years ago I was privileged to meet Leah in London. I saw both Nancy and Dick in her, it was such a lovely sense that actually no one really goes. Dick is literally part of Leah's DNA and her lovely eyes and her smile. For the rest of us who knew him, he can't be gone as long as we remember. We all remember in myriad ways, and thanks to Wayne, some of those memories can be caught and shone again, to cheer us or make us smile or make us glad that we had the extraordinary privilege of being part of Dick's life for a little while or longer.

Dick's life impacted us all, we remember a short life lived with enormous passion and energy and filled to the brim. I personally am so grateful for spending time with that bright, clever, loyal, determined, stubborn, funny, kind, impossible, and extraordinary young man, Dick Barad.

Appendix P

Remembrances from Dick's friends

From Bob Moncrief (January 31, 2011)

Bang, you're dead!

Dickie Barad and I were probably four or five when we met. Our families lived a field apart and our fathers had met and decided to join an "Indian Guides" tribe, which at the time was a father-and-son organization in which the boys could be pre-school age. I was Dickie's age, and David was my older brother Bill's age.

Everyone chose Indian names. I was "Short Bow," a good enough name. Dickie and David's names, however, seemed to portend greatness. They had great botanical names that signified majesty and exceptionalism, names like "Sequoia," and "Saguaro." This regal semiology was later reaffirmed at Camp Spears, in the Poconos, when after a night of poker, the fathers elected Dr. Jerry Barad chief of the tribe; by extension bestowing upon David and Dickie each the status of "savage prince."

Though in the mid-1950s pre-school had not yet entered the zeitgeist, Indian Guide meetings always featured some sort of instruction and structured activity. For example, Stuart Bachelor's father worked for Stangl Pottery (in Flemington) and brought in green ware dishes for us to paint.

However interesting that may have been to preschool boys, it was the unstructured play that often was more memorable. Dickie and David had many play dates with my brother Bill and me. And when at our house, the play was invariably about warfare. Bill and I had toy guns and were constantly lobbying our parents to increase the arsenals of our military-industrial complex.

When David and Dickie came over, we pressured them to join us in pretending to kill each other in endless scenarios that were as historically correct and physically plausible as Bill and I could make them. In our war gaming conversation, the word "authentic" was uttered frequently and with reverence.

The Barad boys did not share our blood lust, preferring more constructive pursuits such as building tree houses, concocting with chemistry sets, or making studies in areas as varied as reptilia, the solar system, and Dr. Barad's photo journals of naked pregnant women. Nevertheless, David and Dickie went to war in order to humor us, but only up to some point at which one of them would end the game, often as not with some passively satirical statement of "inauthenticity."

For example, I remember an argument over who was shot and who was not. I yelled at Dickie, "You're dead! I shot you!" He smiled and rejoined, "The bullet went right through me, made a u-turn, and shot you!" ... Game over.

Moby-Dickie

Dickie Barad and I slept together one night in an ancient double bed when we were eight years old. I had been invited for a sleepover that was to be more intimate than anticipated. I wasn't quite expecting or prepared to sleep in the same bed. Up to that point I had shared a room with my brothers but had never shared a bed with another boy.

I don't remember how the sleeping arrangements were announced but I remember that it was all matter of fact. Mrs. Barad put us to bed and Dickie didn't seem to think it odd. I was outside my comfort zone and trying not to let it show.

I was as trepidatious as Ishmael sharing a boardinghouse bed with Queequeg, the tattooed cannibal. To be fair, though Dickie was a much more congenial and far less ominous character than was Melville's merchant of shrunken heads, Moshe did have proclivities and enterprises nearly as exotic. He loved snakes, horny toads, salamanders, crawdads, and was happy to get his hands on anything that slithers, squirts or barks.

This cozy sleepover wasn't the first time the Barads had surprised me. They were in many ways exotic to my otherwise conventional experience. Their house was filled with unusual plants, live reptiles, and Dr. Barad's photographs from India and Africa.

I've often wondered how our disparate families became friends.

The Barads were international, exurban, and expansive while we Moncriefs must have seemed parochial, white bread conventional, and bucolic. We had the good fortune of their friendship certainly because Dick and I were school chums. But also because my father, though reserved, was, like Dr. Barad, an intellectual. The two men shared a serious interest in agriculture. Both had been seared in the fires of war and had now again embraced life in the postwar boom. Throughout the '50s our families were within walking distance, one field apart.

My night in bed with Dickie would have been in the early sixties, not long after the Barads had moved from the Ringoes house. While their new house near Sergeantsville was still under construction they made camp a few steps down the hill in an existing farm house that is still standing. This massive, once proud multilevel structure, though it had become drafty and crumbling, yet soldiered on with patched plumbing and electricity to sustain the vibrant young family.

So here we were in bed, me feeling confused, unformed and discomfited that another boy's body should be so close just inches away under the covers. Dickie began to make quiet conversation, just as we might have done on the school bus or anywhere else. Eventually my discomfort receded and what came forward was a sweet deepening intimacy and trust. Moshe had shown me his gentle, self-assured powers of guidance. Throughout our friendship my sense was that there was something princely in his behavior, that he might have been (as was Queequeg) the son of a king.

From Michael Zweig (August 28, 2011):

THE BEST OF US

I finally made the time to write this remembrance as Hurricane Irene bore down on us from above. Then I recalled that other day – the day of my friend Dick Barad's funeral, driving northward from New York City, fleeing the onslaught of another Hurricane, Gloria. Memories of Dick still flicker across my mental video screen with a frequency that is surprising given the distance in years we have all now travelled since his death. Several times a year, at least, something reminds me of Dick. Usually it's something I would have liked him to see, or to have experienced with me: my son Ami's wedding; Obama's election; my picture in the New York Times; our friend Joel receiving the Thurgood Marshall award for excellence in criminal defense work – commemorating Joel's efforts in helping to free innocent people, saving their lives. Usually, it's coupled with the thought "Dick would have been proud," accompanied by a conjured vision of that special, remarkable smile – the slight grin, Madonna-like, that only Dick could carry off. Let me see if I can describe it: shy, subtle, approving. He would affect this almost priestly distance with that all-knowing, almost beatific smile, always accompanied by that signature sparkle in his eyes. The light within his soul shining so brightly, now forever extinguished except in our collective memories.

It is extraordinary that, although Dick passed away over 25 years ago, he remains, among our group of friends, someone who we continue to measure ourselves by – and whose standards and expectations we continue to strive to meet. And when we do, we can sometimes see, in our mind's eye, that gorgeous smile once again. He was, as we have become fond of saying in recent years, the "best of us." In remembering him, however, let's cut this man down to earthly size, as he was hardly a saint, nor we his disciples. I met Dick Barad a few days into my freshman year at Cornell University. Thrown together by fate, and the dorm lottery, we lived on the same floor of Clara Dickson Hall – I, in my single room, just a few doors down from his.

It was the first year for "co-ed" dorms at Clara Dickson – Clara undoubtedly would have turned over face down in her grave if she saw the east wing of her building so transformed – populated by still pimply, hormone-crazed and wide-eyed "Big Red" boys. Dick lived in a "double" that was really a triple, owing to his good friend (and roommate) Bill Johnson's having brought his girlfriend, B.J. along with him from New Jersey.

B.J. and Bill, along with Dick, formed an impossible threesome that made sense only by the logic of a group of 18-year olds. Dick's room soon proved to be the place to be.

Dick was in the library most of the time anyway, for he was

pre-med, and studied more intently, and with more focus than any of us, and we studied a lot, to be sure, typically at least from 7 to 12 midnight, when the library finally closed.

All of us, to some degree, experienced our freshman year from Dick's vantage point. After studying (and sometimes before, and during) the guitars would fly out, and a Dick/Bill jam session would flow. During these sessions, Dick, in particular, achieved a mellow state, carefully arranging the frets on his acoustic guitar and playing the music of the day – Dave Bromberg and Hot Tuna, Happy Traum, James Taylor and Paul Simon. B.J. would sing along; and yes, Bill and B.J. would always have a joint to share, if you wished to partake, making their room, truly, the hippest place on the floor. It was from there that we decided what demonstrations to attend, what concerts to make the trek to, and what to do with our lives. There are so many memories from that time – now reappearing in fragments that episodically emerge:

* The days, weeks and months of trudging to and from the library to work, each of us in isolated "study carrels" from which we would escape at midnight, trudging back to our dorm room, amidst the snow, ice and cold of the typical Ithaca winter (and fall and spring);

* Our first "glasses" of wine ("Boone's Farm" and "Cold Duck") -- actually best drunk directly from the bottle, as we sat atop Cornell's stone walls;

* Seeing Dick's A (or A-) and my C (a first) on our initial biology "prelim" test -- my first inkling, perhaps that although I might study as much, and almost as hard, as Dick, my future as pre-med seemed far less certain.

* Seeing Dick excuse himself, in almost monk-like style, from our weekly, desperate searches for live young (preferably "cute") females, within the confines of Ithaca College, then expanding our scope to Keuka and Wells Colleges. Cornell men, at that time, greatly out-numbered its women, and this left most of us with few options. Dick needed none of that, for he was already in a long-term relationship with a mysterious, beautiful woman, Jackie Herbert, for whom he was saving himself. Jackie, an interior design student, lived far away in London – they had met, I think, on a student exchange program in high school. Christmas was Dick's shot at seeing her, and Dick kept his eye on that ball,

smiling empathetically, but eschewing our obsession with the hunt for women, and our weekend jaunts.

During the middle of sophomore year, Dick and I became roommates -- when we rescued him from an untenable living situation. At the conclusion of freshman year, Dick had committed to living again with Bill and B.J. and one or two other "friends of Bill's" in a grimy apartment deep within the bowels of Ithaca's "College Town." But throughout the fall, the apartment, for some reason, required renovation work which caused the apartment to be without heat most of the time and resulted in the appearance of workers, wielding large hydraulic drills, attacking the concrete floor of the apartment at 7 a.m. Dick soon realized that these disruptions (along with the distractions of Bill – who was soon to become the first drop-out in our group) were in conflict with his demanding pre-med course of study.

So, we added a bed, and Dick moved in with me – to the second floor of 505 Wyckoff Avenue and the relative calm of Cayuga Heights. Our bucolic neighborhood was composed of frat houses, family and faculty homes, and many student dwellings.

The room rent was a whopping $70, which Dick and I split at $35 apiece. Our roommate Danny walked through our room to get to his, but no matter. We soon settled into a routine, cooking together, having dinner at 6, them making the communal trudge, over the glorious (but suicide-attracting) suspension bridge which spanned one of Cornell's infamous gorges, connecting Cayuga Heights with the Cornell campus mainland.

Some nights, to save time and trouble, we would splurge and eat at the "Cosmo" diner in College Town, where $3.00 would buy you a full and satisfying meal in 30 minutes or less – moussaka, lasagna, stews of all kinds, and yes, we felt very "cosmopolitan" in doing so. I, in particular, was not used to eating out in a restaurant, or to being "served," so it was a pleasant novelty (all too soon to become a past-time) for me.

A big night out meant that six to eight of us would migrate, like starved animals, to Howard Johnson for their Wednesday night "all you can eat" fish fry, for $2.99. In that orange-roofed emporium we would congregate around one long table and devour plate after plate of fried fish, French fries and cole slaw, piling up, one after another, the serving platters in the middle of the table until the stack grew embarrassingly large. To management's credit, while they may have scowled a bit, they never threw us out. No wonder Howard Johnson, once an icon of American life, went out of business.

Oh, did I mention that the only way we could get to Howard Johnson was by car – Dick's car, to be exact? Yes, my roommate had a car, which cemented his popularity. And better yet, it was an eminently serviceable, fairly ancient, Peugeot 505, a classy vehicle. Light blue and only slightly rusted, the car held 5 or 6 (or 8 or 9, if need be) and soon became our "go-to" vehicle for all types of excursions up (and down) Lake Cayuga and Ithaca's environs – our ticket to the outside world.

At the outset of our junior year, I met Dick at his home in Flemington so he could give me a lift to school. He had decided to bring his bicycle to Ithaca, to exercise but mainly to go to class in the far off reaches of the Cornell campus. We lashed his bike to the back of the car, and proceeded north on Route 81, soon becoming lost in conversation and the radio's blare. Several times during the trip, we both smelled something burning, and pulled over to check the car, opening the hood as if we would know what to do, but finding no obvious fires, continued onward. It was only when we rolled up to 505 Wyckoff Avenue and went to unpack our stuff from the trunk that we realized why the burning smell had stayed with us all the way to Ithaca. Dick's bicycle tire was in the direct path of the Peugeot's exhaust, and was melted straight through. While the beauty of that car was its "low-slung" appearance, it was apparently less than ideal for hauling bicycles.

There were numerous road-trips together to SUNY at Cortland to see the Grateful Dead, to Boston for the "Beantown" hockey tournament (much of which was lost in a haze of pre-game partying), and to Washington D.C. for a massive anti-war demonstration on the Mall. In Ithaca, we would, if feeling financially secure, journey together to the Stagecoach Inn for the one Old Grand Dad bourbon (on the rocks) that we could afford. Sporting events at Cornell were a bit of an after-thought, but we were lucky enough to experience together, in our freshman year, the glory days of Ed Marinaro, the country's leading tailback, and the exciting Cornell hockey team, then a national power, taking on B.U., B.C., R.P.I., Clarkson and Saint Lawrence, for national supremacy.

My legal career began, to some degree, on Dick's watch and with his support. Our junior year marked the beginning of Nixon's wage/price controls. No matter how much we detested Nixon -- and we did -- Nixon's draconian, anti-inflation price controls prohibited any rent increases, and this was extremely useful when your landlord has just decided to raise the monthly rent for your two bedroom from $135 to $200. At that time, the only person less popular on college campuses than Nixon, the police, and ROTC student officers were landlords. And thus followed my first legal foray and first victory ever, for Dick and myself, successfully appealing (to the Price and Wage Control Board in Buffalo) our landlord's unlawful rent increase. Our landlord was named Banfield, and Dick would, in fits of pique when there was no heat or hot water call him "Banbrains." He exulted to me after my victory: "you really beat his Banbrains in."

Dick would, as did the rest of us, spend a great deal of time between classes at the two student-run coffee houses – Temple of Zeus in the Arts & Sciences quad or the Green Dragon, in the Architecture School. Although we did not know it, these were both precursors in spirit and substance to Starbucks – where you would go to do work, socialize, listen to music, and occasionally have a cup of coffee. Most of all, it was a place for us to debate political issues, to rationalize our non-membership in radical student groups such as SDS, and to chill.

By 1972, our two bedroom became conjoined through self-help with the adjacent (mirror image) two bedroom apartment on the same floor occupied by our closest friends and comrades. Yes, it's true, Banbrains, we knocked the wall down between the apartments so that we could move readily back and forth. It was all about flow. This fortunately made the entire second floor of the house the ideal, sprawling party space and we decided to exploit this for a blowout Election Eve party.

Dick and I truly believed (which shows you the height of both our delusion and seclusion) that George McGovern (from South Dakota of all places) stood a good chance at defeating the evil, tricky Dick Nixon. Dick Barad (the good Dick) was, as much as anyone, outraged by the atrocities and insanity of the Vietnam War. We both just assumed the rest of the country would also see the light. Ah, for the unreality of youth. As the returns came in, and it became apparent through the early evening (7 p.m.?) that McGovern would win just one (Massachusetts?) state in 50, our despair reached new lows. Dick and I (and our merry band) proceeded to drink, and drink, and drink until the night grew long, and morning almost broke. We felt no better in the morning, indeed far worse, but at least we felt that we had suitably commemorated a dark day in American history.

Our senior year was marked by widespread communal living with the opposite sex -- all except Dick, who was still saving himself. We lived, relatively harmoniously, in a 7 bedroom 19th century colonial at the foot of Hudson Street in downtown Ithaca. Dick's Peugeot was key for getting us (way up hill) to class in the morning; if he left before us, it meant hitching up the hill, which was de rigueur in those days -- a forerunner, perhaps, of HOV lanes. It was at Hudson Street that Dick and I perfected our cooking skills (Army style) cooking for the masses and presiding with others over daily dinners cooked from scratch -- the old standbys of lasagna, chili and spaghetti.

I graduated from Cornell a semester early, missing Dick's period of agonizing as to which medical school (unbelievably competitive at the time) would accept him. With his father in medicine, and his older brother on the way there, Dick undoubtedly felt no small amount of pressure to succeed. We told him that if he did not deserve admission to med school, no one did. He did get in finally, and in typical Dick fashion, worked extremely hard, so much so that I barely saw him during our first year of graduate school. Yes, I had given up the pursuit of medicine, dallied in my junior year with clinical psychology then, catapulted by my dramatic legal victory over the evil Banbrains, gravitated to law school.

We remained close friends, believing then, as only the immortal youth do, that we would have the rest of our lives to laugh, relax and throw Frisbees to each other, forever.

We attended each other's weddings. He knew my wife Michelle well (no, not in that sense). Michelle remembers his kindness when, following an off-campus celebration where we had too much to drink, he held her hair back as she leaned to the side of the road and puked her guts out. That image – reflecting Dick's gentleness, his thoughtfulness, and valor, still endures.

Dick and Nancy's wedding was also a classic. No catering hall for them; instead, the park-like surroundings of Nancy's family's southern New Jersey farm. And I mean farm – acres and acres of cornfields, and hay, and manure. And a glorious wedding, that is, until the darkest of storm clouds emerged, almost tornado-like, to puncture the stillness and calm of that scene.

To this day, I wonder if that was a harbinger of later storm clouds to come -- that call I received from Dick sharing with me personally that his recurrent headaches were in fact a brain tumor. How could this friend, who had always done just the right thing, have drawn this card? This was far worse than our poor draft lottery numbers, or a mediocre grade on a prelim. When Dick told me this, I thought of the cruel irony of his finishing an idealistic Peace Corps-like stint in Africa with Nancy, his having established a promising family medical practice, again with Nancy, in Brattleboro, [sic.] Vermont and the recent birth of his beloved Leah, who had played so happily with her contemporary Ami on their visits together, in Vermont and the Berkshires.

This was just a temporary setback, an inconvenience, I convinced myself, there was no way God, or the fates could allow this bright light, and soul, to be extinguished. But I was wrong. I saw the only man I ever truly loved wither and then lie dying before me and my main thought was "welcome to the real world."

Dick's passing left a missing link in our chain of friends that was never replaced. In his own way, Dick's was a full (if tragically shortened) life. In his short time, he showed us what it was to live a useful, meaningful life. He was not one to sweat the small stuff, even before it became in vogue. To this day, I still see his quizzical, quiet smile, his slightly approving (and disapproving) look as I flirted with his beautiful sister Dot, his intensity and focus and drive, and the quiet satisfaction he displayed just tossing the Frisbee back and forth as the sun set (as it should) over Sunset Park in Cayuga Heights. How cheated we were by his death. How gifted by his life.

- Michael Zweig (August 28, 2011), Becket, Massachusetts

From Tom Vaughan:

I'm not sure what words I can find. Mostly I just "see" Dick in pictures in my mind. Serious (usually), somewhat earnest, and often with a very slight smile looking like it is about to come out. Always reading, unless he had a camera in his hand. Gentle and thoughtful, but with a sly sense of humor that often caught me by surprise. His damn car! The sky blue Peugeot that was rusted out and sometimes ran. Except when it was 20 degrees below zero outside of the "Straight." Dick under the hood spraying something into the carburetor that would work magic. But we needed that car! Seeing their farmhouse -- he was proud and excited about their future. Later, walking to his radiation appointment at Mass General, a resolute expression on his face. A surprising calm. Don't know how he did it. Near death... watching Leah crawl on him and wondering why he couldn't play anymore.

We were fortunate to meet Leah a few years ago in Seattle. A beautiful and interesting young woman. Dick would have been very proud (in his quiet way.)

Appendix Q

Postings from a Facebook page called "You know you were a friend of Dick Barad's because you remember when he...."

Bob Moncrief remembers, "In I think it was 1966, Dick and David and my brother Bill and I decided to form a jug band for the Hunterdon Central High School *Devil's Cabaret*, the annual talent show. On the day we gathered to decide what music to play, Dick and David showed up with stuff I'd not yet heard of, old clay 78s of Robert Johnson. Lead Belly, and Bessie Smith. I think the Barad boys carried us musically. The rest was burlesque. Our entrance was through an outhouse upstage. And I remember we wore our father's old hats from the 1940s, which we'd soaked overnight and then stretched on bed posts for a look influenced by Al Capp and Big Daddy Roth."

Alan Goodman (HCHS '70 Senior Class President) remembers, "I was at the Barad's, probably 1969 or early 1970. Someone -- a friend or relative -- had given them a box of used record albums. I was looking through them. 'Take anything you want,' Dick told me. I didn't own many records at the time. I picked out Miles Davis, *Milestones,* from 1958. I didn't know it at the time, but it is an amazing record of Class A superstars, with both Cannonball Adderley AND John Coltrane plus Philly Joe Jones, Red Garland and Paul Chambers. Easily one of the best he ever recorded and transitional for Miles because it contained some of the bebop for which he was first known, and some of the cool vibe he was starting to hear.

Milestones was my first real jazz record. Eventually I had close to 10,000, including every album Miles ever recorded. When it was time to acknowledge I was a grown up and that I shared the apartment with my wife, I started selling them all off. I kept, maybe, 80 -- stashed away in my man cave where I keep a working turntable. All the Miles records are on the shelf to this day. I could pick any three at random for my desert island discs, and be happy all my life. I still play that same copy of *Milestone*s, and can sing along with all the solos I've heard it so often. And whenever I play it, I think of Dick's generosity and the passion it helped foster.

Debbie Hooper remembers, "We moved to Delaware Township during the second half of grade 6. I remember in 7th grade going to a get-together at the Barad's, don't recall the occasion. I met the monkey, a boa who crawled my arm, and the boa food! I was impressed! A unique event!

Cynthia Jason Montague (HCHS '70) remembered "Dick was my next-door neighbor and friend. One day he asked me out, and I said no. It was no big deal, but I have always regretted that I never explored more than a friendship with him."

Donna Bettner Hand (HCHS '71) remembers, "I was a freshman

and scared to death; I couldn't for the life of me open my locker, which was by the gym. The more I tried, the more my hand shook and I knew I'd be late to class. A very nice-looking fellow said, 'Here, let me help.' He was dressed in gym clothes. A flick of the wrist and my locker opened. I thanked him profusely, he said no problem and that I should watch out for the 'sky hooks.' I didn't know it that first week of school, but it was Dick."

Pam Motz remembers, "He took me on my first date to a 'Small Fry' dance at Delaware Township School."

Alan Bush (HCHS '70) remembers, "Dick was in different social and school classes than myself. One winter evening I was invited to sled riding at Dick's house. (The) Barad's had the best homemade sled course I had ever seen. Forty-five years later I still think of how welcome I felt. One act of friendship is still remembered and keeps Dick with me."

Appendix R

e-mails on Dick's 50th birthday

April 21, 2002
To: all the Barads
From: Dot Barad
Subject: To celebrate Dick's 50th birthday

Dear Family,

It's important to celebrate the good of life.
Today is April 21, it's Dick's 50th... hard to believe. In keeping with this thought, go out today and appreciate the daffodils.
For the Berkeley boys and the African members of the clan: If it is not daffodil season in your zone find something you love equally as well.
XXOX
much love,
Dot

(Her brother Bob wrote this reply:)

Dot,

Thanks for the thought and the courage of sharing it.
I bet Dick would have been one of the finest 50-year-olds ever grown. He would also have been a great friend in times of trouble or joy.
I miss him a lot.

Love,
--Bob

Appendix S

The Barad/Krival Family History

Chaim and Chana Blick Kryvula emigrated from the Ukraine with their two young daughters Brana (Bessie) and Rejza (Rose) and their two-month-old son Uszer in February, 1921, during one of the pogroms against the Jews. The five of them arrived at Ellis Island on March 3, 1921, but baby Uszer was sent into quarantine for an unspecified illness and died two weeks later, on March 18.

Chaim and Chana and their two surviving daughters moved to Newark, New Jersey, into an apartment in the back of a store with the help of Chana's brother, Abe Blick, who had emigrated before World War I when he fled the Ukraine to keep from being drafted into the Kaiser's army.

Two years later, in 1923, Chana gave birth to Beatrice Miriam Krival (as the last name was Anglicized). Some years later, the Krival family moved to Bensonhurst into a three-story house at 6417 17th Avenue and opened a grocery store on the ground floor. Rose would eventually live on the second floor of the house while her sisters and parents lived on the third floor.

The Barad name is most likely a patronymic for "Ben Reb David" (son of Reb David, "Reb" translating to "beloved."). The Russian Czar appears to have required last names sometime in the 19th century and the Jews obliged him. "Barad" is also a Hebrew word meaning "hail" (like ice that falls from the sky) and is one of the 10 plagues mentioned during the Passover Seder.

David Nathan Barad dabbled in real estate investments near the end of the 19th century, and one of those purchases led the family to relocate to Brooklyn, New York, where they lived in a three-story brownstone on Eastern Parkway as well as owning a house at the beach. Soon, however, he bought a double lot on Coleridge Street in the Manhattan Beach section of Brooklyn. He built a house for his family and would eventually give the other lot to his oldest daughter, Victoria. David was fascinated with automobiles and was reportedly the first to own one on their block, including a Stanley Steamer.

Two papers that David Barad, Ph.D. published in 1892 (Zur Kenntniss der [Beta]-Alkyl-[Alpha]-Phenyl-phenmiazine and Zur Kenntniss der B-Alkyl-&-Phenylphenmiazine) can still be found on the internet. (See Adele's "family history" in Appendix T.) David and Adele's son Alexander would marry Mildred Hess (born November 14, 1900) of Brooklyn, and they settled in Manhattan Beach at 218 Beaumont Street, one block west of Coleridge Street. (The streets in Manhattan Beach run alphabetically as they move eastward: Amherst, Beaumont, Coleridge, etc.).

It was at the Beaumont Street house that Gerald (Jerry) Samuel Barad, their only child, would be born on March 22, 1923. When Jerry was about four or five years old, Alex and Mildred moved with their young son to Belgium. At the time, Alex was a buyer and importer of diamonds and semi-precious stones. The family spent two years in Belgium and France.

When they came back to Brooklyn, Jerry could only speak French which caused him some problems with the local children in and around Beaumont Street, calling him "Frenchy" and picking on him. In his own words, he quickly learned English and forgot everything about the French language.

Alex had earned a degree in chemical engineering at New York University, but he was destined to be an entrepreneur. They returned from Europe at the height of the Great Depression, and some of the business dealings Alex became involved with included importing feather ornaments, manufacturing chocolate, selling butter and eggs, and finally settling in as a commodities trader. One business Alex worked at was as an egg distributor. He would buy eggs wholesale, package them by dozens in cartons and sell them to retail establishments. Jerry remembers being 10 or 11 years old and having a retail egg route: he would take some of the packages of eggs and deliver them to homes on his bicycle along his own "route." His father ventured as far as Flemington, New Jersey, some 60 miles west of Brooklyn to buy his eggs in bulk. (Flemington would later play a large role in the Barad family history).

Some of the other ventures that Alex pursued included importing wholesale butter. At the time, the rule by U.S. Customs was that imported butter of at least 80% butterfat was charged a higher duty rate than those with a lower butterfat content. Alex used his chemical engineering degree to develop a butter product with only 75% butterfat and he would mix it with some other ingredient, like chocolate. Then he would give the product a name and get it declared an import product at a lower duty fee. He would then send the recipe to a company overseas and order a boatload of the product to be imported. When the product arrived, Alex would pay the lower duty fee and then deliver the butter to bakeries and ice cream companies and make a tidy profit.

Appendix T

Great-Aunt Adele Barad's Family History (date unknown)

Fragments of memories of my grandparents have remained with me over the years. These bits and pieces plus data gleaned from U.S. Census records, yellowed album photos, and some recollections of my uncle Emil written before he died, are all the family history I have. Too late to regret that I didn't ask more questions when I was growing up, and now there is no one left to ask. Lest it all disappear with me, I will try to get a coherent picture down on paper.

A biography *Nazimova* by Gavin Lambert, published in 1997, has added some new information to my meager store of knowledge about my ancestors. The actress Alla Nazimova, (born Adele Leventon, same name as my grandmother) was grandmother's cousin. According to the author, whose source was autobiographical notes by Alla, their common grandfather was an uneducated miller who had five children. His children lived a hard and deprived life with a lot of drudgery after being sent for an elementary education at a synagogue school. At the age of 16, the oldest, Lyev, left home, supporting himself by tutoring and eventually put himself through a medical education at the University of Kiev. He was able to help his brothers and sister get a university education. Isaac became a lawyer. Yakov, Alla's father got a degree in chemistry but struggled as a pharmacist's assistant. Sister Lysenka became a surgeon. My grandmother's father, Ilya was recorded in Alla's notes as being a farmer - a big surprise to me, as I had heard many times that he was a pharmacist, a respected professional in the town of Yedintsy. This discrepancy has made me cautious about believing everything Nazimova had to say about her youth. Perhaps tales of her despicably cruel father are exaggerated. Who knows?

One thing she wrote that I'd like to believe is that the summers she spent with my grandmother's family was the closest thing to a real family life she had ever known. Adele Leventon, my mother's mother was born in 1871 in Yedintsy, Bessarabia. Bessarabia is now part of the republic of Moldova, having come full circle. Over the centuries, it has been in succession, a principality, part of the Ottoman Empire, Russian, Romanian, part of the U.S.S. R called Moldavia, and now Moldova again.

Her mother's name was Sofia Ornstein. The family must have been quite assimilated because Adele knew no Yiddish and was not at all observant, or even familiar with Judaism. However, that did not protect her from discrimination in her educational opportunities; she had to leave the country for university education. Hers was a highly-educated family for their time and place, as she had a sister, (Victoria or Masha) who became a physician, emigrating to Germany after marrying a fellow medical student, and a brother, (Boris or Bubchik) who was a mining engineer in Siberia. Another brother, Alexander, had a son by the same name called Shura who came to this country in 1922 with his very beautiful wife Katya. He was a gifted violinist and became concertmaster of the Rochester Philharmonic Orchestra. He was also a fine photographer and won many prizes for his portraits, one being of his son Boris. The portrait of a youngster in a fur hat was widely used in Kodak advertising and I was very proud, as a child, to see my second cousin's face looking out at me from store windows and magazine pages.

Adele's cousin Alla Nazimova was a renowned stage actress, known for her dramatic roles, particularly Ibsen. I believe I saw her on the stage late in life in Eugene O'Neil's *Mourning Becomes Electra*. Fame and wealth and popular acclaim came to her through her years in Hollywood. But the roles she played as a sex siren did not do justice to her dramatic ability.

Gavin Lambert says that the Leventon family traced its ancestry to the Levanderas, Sephardic Jews of medieval Spain. That's news to me. I have written to him asking for documentation but have not received a reply yet.

Back to Zurich and the University where Adele met fellow student, David Nathan Barad, born in 1869 in Odessa. He came from a more typical Jewish background, knowing Yiddish, and having first-hand experience with violent anti-Semitism. I remember him saying that during the pogroms against the Jews in Odessa, his family had to put a cross on their door to escape harm. I don't know if his family was observant, but he was a socialist and rejected religion.

David emigrated to the United States in 1892, on the promise of a job as a chemist in Cleveland from an American he had met in Zurich. The job turned out to be a phantom, and not knowing the language, he had to take anything just to keep alive. So, his first job was as a "barker" outside a market in a Jewish neighborhood. Adele joined him two years later, and they were married. Eventually, he got work in his field in Philadelphia, where my mother Victoria was born in 1895. But, as the story goes, Adele became homesick, so pregnant with Alexander, they went back to Russia.

I don't know if they had planned to stay, but if they did, the reception David received would have caused them to reconsider. He was arrested and jailed because of "revolutionary" activities he had taken part in as a student. The "crime" was in printing anti-government literature - something his mother had suspected when she saw his constantly ink-stained hands. My mother had vague memories of visiting in jail, and the embarrassment of being taken to the bathroom under armed guard. Eventually he was released, due to string-pulling, or maybe palm-greasing, by his mother.

I remember one earlier narrow escape from the law that my grandfather had as a young student radical. He told me that he had been detained by the police, who noticed that he had a copy of Karl Marx's *Das Kapital*. Translating the title, the police officer put his own interpretation of the meaning, apparently having no idea of what the book was about, "Oh", he said. "Just like a Jew, always wanting to make money!" If he knew that the writings were about socialism, he wouldn't have gotten off so easy.

As to my grandfather's siblings, to quote my Uncle Emil: "He had two sisters. Polya married a man by the name of Zollozitzer who abandoned her and their two little girls. My mother told me that Polya had been a very pretty young girl and Zollo was a lady killer. One of the girls died quite young (about five years old). The other was Ida who worked for many years in the office of Gimble's Department Store in New York. She married a postal clerk, last name Sunshine. He was an addicted horse-player who skipped town when his bookie told him to pay up or else. He turned up in the Post Office in Jacksonville, Florida and he and Ida resumed their relationship. There followed another skip, and Ida returned to Brooklyn to live with her mother. My father's other sister became (of all things!) a dentist in (of all places!) Alexandria, Egypt."

Alexander was born in Russia in 1897 and the family returned to the U.S., never to see Russia again. Adele was always nostalgic for Yedintsy. I remember, in my teen years, after she had moved from place to place, she still kept an etching of her home in Bessarabia hanging on the wall. After a gap of eight years, another pair of children were born: Vera in 1905 and Emil in 1908, making a nice symmetry of older and younger boy-girl siblings.

At some point, David was chief chemist for the Anspacher Paint Company. The story goes that they made the green paint that covered all the U.S. mail boxes, and that he would often come home with his beard stained green. But he dabbled in real estate, and eventually made it his full-time occupation. He must have done very well with his investment in real estate because the Barads led a very comfortable life. By the time I was born, they lived in a three-story brownstone on Eastern Parkway, Brooklyn and had a summer house on beach (sic).

David was fascinated by automobiles and was the first on the block to own one. From then on it was continuous car ownership for the rest of his life. I remember the Stanley Steamer, which was notable because it had trouble negotiating steep hills, and there were times when wood blocks had to be placed behind the rear wheels, to keep the car from rolling backwards, when trying to start it after it had stalled on an incline.

There was more buying and selling of houses, but the one I remember was the house in Manhattan Beach, which combined the best of both locations, suburbia AND the beach. That house on Coleridge Street had a double lot, and later, one lot was given to my parents for our house. There were also trips to Europe. (When I was growing up) I had been told many times by my grandmother that when I turned 16, she would take me to Europe. But, alas when that time came, times and circumstances had changed and the promise was not mentioned.

In spite of their affluence and capitalistic tendencies, the family never gave up its support of socialism. They were very anti-war, during the first World War, much to the scorn of some of their friends. They were faithful supporters of Eugene Debs and then Norman Thomas for president, until the campaign of Franklin Roosevelt, and from then on they were New Dealers.

My uncle Alex trained as a chemist at New York University, but his life work was in various business enterprises. The earliest one I remember involved importing feather ornaments. He and his wife Mildred (Hess) and their only child Gerald spent some time living in France. Enough time for Jerry to come back speaking French as a child of four or five (actually, he was six). Alex went on to establish other businesses. One of them, to my delight, chocolate. Then butter and eggs. Commodities dealing became his final niche. And at home, I remember him being a fine, imaginative cook, a quality he passed on to Jerry.

He was an inventive person since childhood, sometimes putting his technical expertise to mischievous use. The story handed down was that when he was a teen-ager, he wired the toilet used by the maid so that she got a shock when she urinated.

Emil had an engineering college education at Rensselaer Polytechnic Institute in Troy, New York. I don't know whether he stayed to get his degree, but while he was there he fell in love with Lillian Symansky who was from a Troy family. They married and moved in with my grandparents who were now living in a small apartment in Flatbush. These were unfortunate circumstances for a young married man to be finding a career as it was just about the time of the stock market crash and the onset of the Great Depression.

Emil went to law school in Brooklyn, but due to the dismal economic situation, there was no work for lawyers in private practice. He found a position as Clerk of the Surrogate Court in the Borough of Queens and made that his career for the rest of his working life. His family was the first of the Barads to leave Brooklyn when they bought a small house in Flushing.

Except for Vera, of course, who led a very peripatetic life. I remember my uncle Emil as being an unsentimental man of few words, but what he said was carefully weighed and taken seriously. An incident is still vivid in my mind when I, the usual fresh and snippy teen-ager, said something unpleasant to my father. I have no idea what it was that I said, but I remember clearly the aftermath. It was in our home, Emil was there.

When I walked to the door as he was leaving, he said quietly to me, "You shouldn't have talked to your father that way." Because it was Emil who said it, tears welled up in my eyes, and I felt embarrassed and ashamed.

Aunt Vera was by far the most colorful of the Barad children. So colorful, that it's hard to know where to begin. I could begin with her name. People close to the family called her "Pussy." As a child I saw nothing strange in that until outsiders hearing it started raising eyebrows. The name stems from the Russian custom of bestowing numerous nicknames on family members. She was not only "Pussy" since babyhood, but "Pussitchka" and "Verushka." My mother was "Massia" and "Massitchka." Emil was "Sikki." There were others but I can't recall them anymore.

Vera seemed to have been born with an adventurous spirit. She never got on the track that took the other family members from college to marriage to raising a family. She did her own thing. And from what I have heard, she caused her parents much pain and anxiety. But oh, did she have a life! She would leave the house in the morning and Grandma, peeking from the window, could see her walking in the opposite direction from school. When she was a bit older, she "borrowed " the car and drove to New Jersey! That was a very daring thing for a young girl to do in the early days of motoring, before there were bridges or tunnels to cross the Hudson. She made an attempt to start higher education, but it didn't last long.

However, writing was her forte. The only job I ever heard her talk about was as a correspondent for a business firm. Writing under a fictitious male name, she developed a friendly pen-pal relationship with some of the letter writers and got carried away with the play acting to a point where she had to develop ploys to avoid meeting her clients when they came to New York. She was always a fantastic story teller, so who knows?

Sometime in the early 1920's, my grandparents took a trip to California. They stayed a while to see whether they would enjoy living there, and whether the climate would be helpful for David's circulatory problem. Apparently, Vera was with them, for while there she met and married a would-be movie actor named Leigh (or Lee) Harris. I have no clues as to the time frame of this whole California episode, but the marriage was not looked upon with favor and was short-lived. As for Leigh Harris, he never got beyond bit parts, and was soon forgotten both in the films and family.

Back in New York, Vera was an habitue of Greenwich Village at the time when it was the foremost meeting place of artists, writers and musicians, particularly of the avant garde sort. Their favorite hang-out was Romany Marie's, called a tea room but more like what we would think of today as a coffee house. Of all the names in that world I might have heard her mention, the only one that sticks is Stuart Davis, the artist. Grandma complained from time to time that when she got up in the morning she never knew what strange man she would find sleeping on the couch. One I remember seeing quite often was a composer named Reichman. He even tried to give me piano lessons, but teaching kids was not his forte.

Sometime during this period, which extended into the thirties, Vera met a naval officer named Mark Clay from Hutchinson, Minnesota, at Romany Marie's. Mark was a very unlikely combination: a navy man from a small Midwest town with an affinity for the arts and a love of Bach. He was a soft-spoken, mild-mannered man who chose the least militaristic branch of the Navy - Supply. He must have passed muster with Romany Marie who could make tourists who stumbled into her place feel very unwelcome.

Eventually Vera and Mark married, and she took up the new role of Navy Wife. One tour of duty took Mark to China where he was stationed on a Yangtze River patrol ship. During this period, the late thirties, China, ostensibly now a Republic, was a battleground for various military factions. Eventually, the Nationalists under Chiang Kai Shek gained control, but the Communists under Mao were constantly challenging them from the North. At the same time, the Japanese had occupied Manchuria and were a threat to this disunited country.

During the previous century, various foreign powers had gained remarkable privileges in China. They had "concessions" in the major cities where their nationals could live as if they were in the home country, not subject to local law. The right of the U.S. Navy to patrol the Yangtze River was one of these privileges. To what purpose, I don't know. Probably to remind the various factions of U.S. interest and power.

Meanwhile Vera was living a comfortable life in what I believe was a British concession in Canton. She played a lot of tennis at "the club." I remember her writing that the unspoken rule was that Chinese could be ball boys, but one never, never played a game with them no matter how accomplished they were. Her letters from China in those days were exciting events for us. We would gather at Grandma's to hear of her latest experiences and impressions. She stayed there until the air raids got too close for comfort and the Navy wives were sent home. One of her letters told how they would all go up on the roof to watch the bombing in the distance. Her letters were worthy of being saved, or even published. But, alas, they have disappeared. After we entered World War II, Mark spent a lot of time at sea, and Vera stayed in Georgia, in the company of other Navy wives, playing tennis and waiting.

At the same time I was in the Women's Army Auxiliary Corps, and rather out of touch. So, I was really shocked to learn that she was divorcing Mark and marrying Vilem Zwillinger whom she met at the Fort Ogelthorpe Hotel. Vilem Zwillinger was a very imposing character. A refugee economist from Czechoslovakia, he had been "undersecretary in charge of the social security system." His whole demeanor was of one who was accustomed to and required the best of everything. I don't know how he could have come here, a refugee, with the means to satisfy all his needs, but he soon spent money as though it were no problem: custom-made shirts from Sulka, ties from Knieze, nothing but the finest.

He and Vera had an apartment on 12th Street, which I remember well because they lent it to us for a while when we were first married. But they soon moved to an apartment on Park Avenue which Vera set about filling with antiques. He tipped the doorman and everybody else lavishly, which seemed to buy him lots of the respect he required. For a number of years, Vera and Willie would rent a big house in Westhampton Beach, Long Island, for the summer. Family members were invited out for a weekend.

One summer Willie got the notion that it would be nice to have a motor boat to putter around the bay. He had no experience with boats, just walked into a dealer and asked for the "best" one and of course ended up with the most expensive mahogany job, which was sold back to the dealer at the end of the season. Jack, a real boating and fishing person, was astonished at his way of shopping. No one like him had ever been in our family before - or since.

Vera could be very generous with money to particular people in need. Jack's sister Rachel is very grateful for the financial aid she received which helped her get through Cornell. Willy made his money in the movie industry. He called himself a financial advisor. And his intuition served him very well for a time. One of his coups was selling old movies to television. Prior to that venture, Hollywood would have nothing to do with television, considering it a threat.

The years from about 1946 to 1962 saw the movie industry going downhill. Box office receipts were falling steadily. It was not only television, but the enormous expense of the studio system which kept actors, writers, directors and all other staff on contract whether or not a film was being made. But collaborating with TV rather than ignoring it was a good financial strategy.

His big mistake was in trying to produce films himself at a time when the movie industry was in such a state of flux. He lost his shirt. But typically of Willy, he had to put up a big front. Life on Park Avenue went on as usual. It was not discovered until after he died in 1960 of rectal cancer how really broke he was. Vera, at the time was suffering from lung cancer (she was a cigarette smoker). What a time to find out that her husband had left her with practically nothing! She died shortly after.

The appearance of importance was a necessary part of Willy's life. He couldn't stand having anything second-rate connected to his name. He gave Jack a chess set once, which was very nice, though not unusual. But he went into a description of how it was hand-carved by a special craftsman somewhere, and on and on and on. After a few years of that sort of thing, we began to wonder how much of his life was real and how much was fantasy.

Vera was someone I had held in awe and admiration since my childhood. Such an exciting life! Such enthralling stories! Her approval mattered to me. If I was made embarrassed or uncomfortable by something she said or did to me, I blamed myself. But from the perspective of adulthood, I took another reading. Her stories were often at the expense of other people, making them look foolish or incompetent. But most often, behind their backs. I later began to feel that she was probably doing the same thing to me when I wasn't there. I stopped sharing anything personal with her. I began to see her as a bitter, self-absorbed woman.

My grandfather lived until about 1943 and my grandmother until 1952, all the time in Brooklyn (which) was also my home until I married. Although they and my family made several moves, we were always physically fairly close. On 22nd street, we lived only two doors away. So, I saw a good deal of them. In later years, it became customary for the family to get together Sundays and play Michigan Rummy. All except Jake, my father, who came but never played cards.

I will try to paint a picture of my grandfather, David, as I remember him in his later years. He was suffering from Buerger's disease, a circulatory problem. This affected his walking to a point where he had to stop every few steps. He had been a very heavy smoker of imported Turkish cigarettes before the diagnosis. When it was recommended that he stop due to his condition, he stopped cold turkey. He had a habit of biting his nails, perhaps to compensate for not smoking. I never saw him actually doing it, but his nails were down to the quick.

Real estate was his livelihood but when the Depression hit, I remember nothing but sighs and heartaches from it. It's hard to imagine today, but the big problem was keeping his apartments filled and rent collected. Apartments were going begging and families (including ours) moved frequently if they could get a better deal somewhere else. Landlords bent over backwards to keep their tenants. New refrigerator? You've got it. Paint job? O.K. One month, two-month concession? Take it! I remember him as being a quiet man who sighed a lot. Probably depressed.

He was a big Brooklyn booster. In spite of all he had seen in the world, he always maintained that you didn't have to go anywhere; we had it all in Brooklyn. He loved Prospect Park. It was beautiful in those days, and we were regulars at the Goldman Band concerts. He was a member of the Brooklyn Academy of Arts and Sciences and had access to the lectures and concerts at the Academy of Music. In an earlier time, he was one of the founding members of the Brooklyn Ethical Culture Society (now the Ethical Humanist Society). And there was the Brooklyn Museum. We had it all in Brooklyn.

Appendix U

Emil Barad recalls family history in a letter to Adele

March 28. 80

Dear Adele:

Sorry we missed your visit. It's always so good to see you both. At about that time we had gone on a six-week trip to Boston, Dubrovnik, Sorrento, Taormina and Rome. The weather again was bad and Lillian had a bad fall just two days before we left for Europe so our movements were quite restricted. Lillian is all better now (from the fall, that is) and we plan to go to Switzerland mid-June to mid-July.

Now down to business. My father was born in Odessa in 1869. When he was in his mid-teens he engaged in revolutionary activity. He was probably printing anti-government stuff. His mother noticed that his hands were stained with printer's ink. She was not surprised when the police came to the house one day to look for him. Fortunately, he was not home and she managed to get word to him to stay away. So, at the age of 16 he became a fugitive and fled to Switzerland, probably with the help of co-conspirators. I don't know how he supported himself there. He entered the Polytechnikum in Zurich and graduated cum laude. From Z he went to the U of Berlin where he received his PhD in chemistry.

In Z he met my mother, who was also a student. I think she attended the university, not the polytech. They enjoyed each other's company very much and took many week-end trips together to Weggis, Rigi, Lucern, etc. There is no new thing under the sun.

He had two sisters. Polia married a man by the name of Zollozitzer who abandoned her and their two little girls. My mother told me that Polia had been a very pretty young girl, and that Zollo was a lady-killer. One of the girls died quite young (about five). The other was Ida who worked for many years in the office of Gimbel's. She married a postal clerk last name Sunshine. He was an addicted horse player who skipped town when his bookie told him to pay up or else. He turned up in the PO in Jacksonville and he and Ida resumed their relationship. There followed another skip and Ida returned to Brooklyn to live with her mother. Last address was 483 Georgia Avenue. After my mother died I sent a check to Polia every month until she died. I haven't heard from Ida since.

My father's other sister became (of all things!) a dentist in (of all places!) Alexandria, Egypt. That's all that I know about her.

My mother had two brothers: Boris (Bubchik) and Alexander (Sasha) and one sister Victoria (Masha). Bubchik was a mining engineer in Siberia. I have a piece of mineral, probably agate, that he sent to my mother from there. Sasha married and they had one child Alexander (Shura) who came to this country with his very beautiful wife Katya in 1922. He was a gifted violinist and became concertmaster of the Rochester Civic Orchestra. He was also a fine photographer and won many prizes, one being for a portrait of his son Boris. I think I recall that it was published in the NY Times. All dead now except Boris Leventon, whereabouts unknown, who would be your second cousin; and Vicki's second once removed.

Masha was in Zurich at the same time as my parents. She studied medicine and became a physician. She married Emil Hoelemann (after whom I was named). He was a physician and practiced in Dresden for many years at Fuerstenplatz 3 I. They had two children, Hans and Hiltrud. Hans was a mathematician. Hiltrud married a teacher. They had a daughter Roswitte.

Yednitz, where my mother was born, is a tiny dot on a large map of Russia. It is in Bessarabia, near Romania. Her father Ilya (translates as Eli) was the town pharmacist. His brother was the father of Alla Nazimova, which would make her my mother's first cousin, your twice-removed, and Vicki's three-times-removed. Alla had a sister whose son, Vladimir, was known as Val Lewton. He was a well-known Hollywood writer.

When my mother died, Pussy took my father's naturalization papers and his diplomas. When she died, I think my sister Vera took the diplomas. My brother took the naturalization papers because he was covered by them, having been born in Russia.

My mother's maiden name was Ornstein.

Well, that's all I can think of now. If anything else comes to mind I'll let you know. I feel like the last of the Mohicans.

> Love,
> Emil

Appendix V

The search for Uncle Uszer

From Bob Barad (December 26, 2005)

None of us ever met Uncle Uszer, but his brief life chronicles a moment in time that changed our lives forever. If he were alive today, Uszer Kryvula would be celebrating his 85th birthday, the last surviving member of the Kryvula-Bleich family who together traveled in the winter months of 1921 from Eastern Europe to America, from the old world to the new, and from persecution to freedom. Uszer, Asher, or Arthur, the anglicized name he would most likely have taken in the United States, was born in December 1920 in the town of Chernyy Ostrov, the only son of my mother's parents, Chaim and Chana Kryvula.

He appears on Chana's Polish passport in the company of his mother and his two European-born sisters Brana (Bessie) and Rejza (Rosie). In the photo, the children's faces appear tightly bundled against the winter cold. In Chana's face we read the worry and exhaustion of that time and place. This was a family fleeing from a war-torn border town, where Jewish heritage was too often deemed a death warrant by the ruling authorities, irrespective of which competing regime held power there. From Chaim and Chana's passports we know the Kryvula family was in Warsaw on 27 January 1921, where they obtained, for a fee of $10 per passport, their visas to come to the United States. One week later, both passports were stamped with transit visas for Belgium.

We next see Uszer's name joined with the nine others in the Kryvula- Bleich group, each name neatly typed on the passenger manifest of the S.S. Kroonland, a ship sailing from Antwerp, Belgium on 17 February 1921, and recorded as arriving at Ellis Island Immigration Station, New York, on 3 March 1921.

The Kroonland manifest does not tell us about their two-week journey, but we know that for Uszer it must have been a harsh one. He is initially listed as entering the ship in good health, but on arrival at Ellis Island he was sent to quarantine. The manifest records his death there 15 days later, with the handwritten note, "Died 3/18/21" and the rubber stamp, "Hospital Discharge".

It is unlikely that my grandparents ever saw the Kroonland manifest. They were immigrants in a country where they did not yet speak the language, their infant son one of the unlucky few who because of weakened health was detained at Ellis Island. On that March day, Chana emerged from quarantine without Uszer, rejoining her waiting husband and two daughters. Together they moved in with relatives who had settled at Newark, New Jersey. Two years later, their youngest child was born there, my mother, Beatrice Miriam Krival.

Fast forward 80 years. Ellis Island is opened to the public as an historic site, and my sister, Dorothy Barad, visits its History Center. Unable to locate our family records in the Center's database, she asks about the island's cemetery where we had learned as children that our uncle was buried in an unmarked grave. "There's no cemetery on Ellis Island", she is told by the staff. It becomes a nagging mystery. What really happened to our uncle, and where was his final resting place? The same question nagged at our Aunt Bessie, who, in the last years of her life as her health faded and her mind wandered, became preoccupied with knowing her brother's fate.

Bessie's death on 19 April 2005, just days after her 92nd birthday, came as my son Richard was preparing for his Bar Mitzvah, an event marking his 13th birthday and his introduction to the responsibilities of Jewish adulthood. As part of this preparation, we had worked together to assemble a family tree documenting his Jewish roots, including Chana, Chaim, and six other Great Grandparents. Because we live in Rome, Italy, and because my job with the United Nations World Food Programme is computer-focused, we relied mostly on information we could find through the Internet.

Our research led us back to the Nathan family web site, where we found a rich depository of Krival family history, including the stories that Bessie had told her son Ronald Nathan of the family's life in Chernyy Ostrov and their journey to America. Here too, our Israeli cousin, Sheila Warshawsky, had posted a message that revealed to us the reason Dot's database search had not been fruitful: Our grandparents had been entered in the Kroonland manifest not as Krival, or Kryvula, but "Krywula", a spelling of their last name unique to that document. Querying Ellis Island's online database was now a simple task. Only five of the more than 12 million immigrants who had landed there between 1892 and 1954 were recorded with the family name "Krywula". One click and there on my computer screen shown Uszer's name, complete with a link to the Kroonland manifest, and the names of his parents, sisters, and maternal grandparents, Bencion and Feiga Blick.

I sent Dorothy the search parameters, and soon after, my observation about the notes next to Uszer's listing at line 23 of the manifest. "If his death was recorded there, shouldn't there also be an official death certificate, and if so, wasn't it important for us to see it?" Dot asked. I went back to the Internet for answers, discovering the story of another infant immigrant, Apollonia Spiegel, who died in quarantine at Ellis Island.

"The Forgotten of Ellis Island", an Internet site dedicated to describing the quarantine experience of Apollonia, Uszer, and so many others, proved a pivotal resource. There I found step-by-step instructions detailing how to request copies of New York City death certificates dating from before 1949.

I passed this reference back to Dot at her Paris, France apartment. She quickly filled in the online form and authorized the New York City Department of Records to make a $15 charge on her credit card. On 25 May 2005, just five weeks after Bessie's death, a copy of Uszer Kyrvula's death certificate arrived in Dot's mailbox in rural upstate New York.

The death certificate was a mine of new information. Through it, we confirmed the date, time, and place of death. But there were also handwritten entries detailing the cause of death, the place and date of burial, and the name and address of the undertaker who performed the burial.

Two phone calls and one hour later, Dot's fax machine printed a second document, Uszer's "Application for Burial" by the "Hebrew Free Burial Association", a charity performing traditional burial rites for Jews who die without the financial resources to pay for these services. Here, written in clear and precise handwriting, was the answer to the question that had remained a mystery for more than 84 years: Uszer's mortal remains lay buried at Grave 79, Row 6, Section 30, of Mount Richmond Cemetery, Staten Island, New York.

Hearing the news, family members expressed sadness that these facts could not have been shared with Bessie just a few weeks earlier, before her death. Perhaps this news of Uszer's final resting place and dignified burial might have brought our dear Aunt Bessie some comfort as she too faced death so many years later.

Perhaps. But I would also like to think that in rejoining her cherished family at the other end of life's journey, Bessie somehow contributed to all of this. It is said that in Jewish tradition there is no direct translation of the English word "luck". Jews speak instead of "mazel," the "drip from above". I would like to think that Bessie, together with all our family's dear and departed ones, sent us that drip from above.

Thank you, Aunt Bessie, we love you, and we miss you.

At 10:08 AM 5/30/2006, Bob wrote an email to UKR-ODESSA-GEN-L@rootsweb.com:

Greetings!

I am a newcomer to this list and a beginner family genealogist. My Great Grandfather David Nathan Barad was born in 1869 in Odessa. US census records indicate he first came to the USA in 1892. He married Adele Leventon of Yedintsy, Moldavia in 1894. They made at least one trip back to Russia, around 1896. My Grandfather, Alexander Barad, was born there on 10 June 1897, before they returned to the USA in 1898.

I have located Ellis Island passenger records for the arrival of David Nathan Barad's mother in 1905. The manifest lists her as Lian/Leah Baradt, aged 60, accompanied by her daughter, Poli Baradt. Polina Barad's 1906 marriage record lists mother Leah and father Nathan. Family history passed down from those times records that there was a second sister, a dentist, name unknown, who settled in Alexandria, Egypt. However, Ellis Island records the arrival of a sister Anna Barad, age 20 in 1904.

Although I have identified the FHL films containing my Great Grandfather's naturalization records, I have not yet been able to access them. Though pleased with the family details I have been able to uncover so far, I think I may be reaching the limits of what USA-based records can offer.

My narrow research objective is to identify the parents of Nathan and Leah who would likely have been born around 1820, possibly in Odessa, but also possibly elsewhere. Austria-Hungary

(Galicia) and Romania both seem like probable places of pre-Odessa family origins, given their number of Barad surnamed records.

From: Anita < anitac47@optonline.net>
Reply-To: UKR-ODESSA-GEN-L@rootsweb.com
To: UKR-ODESSA-GEN-L@rootsweb.com
Subject: Re: [Ukr-Odessa-Gen] Researching Barad and Baradt in Odessa
Date: Tue, 30 May 2006 19:57:59 -0400

Dear Bob,
    Welcome.
    The archives in Odessa have Jewish records from 1875 and the occasional piece of this and that (apologies to Bette Davis). With that in mind, you will not be able (without luck in Galina finding some "this and that"):
 a) Leah's birth (you would need a maiden name), Leah's marriage (unless she married very late for a young Jewish woman of that time--she would have been 35 based on the 1905 arrival at 60 years old--unless you're lucky and she remarried).
b) David Nathan's birth (1869) It is possible you could find Polina's or Anna's birth data (assuming birth around 1875). Or someone's death if it was recorded.
    I have no idea how common the name was in Odessa. That is something you could ask of Galina before the search and therefore search everyone with that name.
    But going back to 1820, well, welcome to my world. I know my great grandfather was born 1820 and I even know his father's name but before that year it is very difficult.

Regards,
Anita Citron

Bob sent the following reply:

Anita,

Thanks for your message. I think the Barad(t) name was uncommon in Odessa, but if Galina were to find records of multiple Barad(t) families in the archives I would be so delighted!!

US records indicate that my Great Great Aunt Polina was born in 1884, so I am hopeful her birth record is in the archive. Also, it would be fantastic to discover the first name of the sister that moved to Alexandria, Egypt. She could have been born or married after 1875, or entered in the 1897 census. Interested to hear from anyone else on the list that has information about family who moved from Odessa to Egypt.

The death record of my Great Great Grandfather Nathan Barad(t) would be a prized discovery, because it could contain the names of his parents, the unknown previous generation. He was certainly alive in 1884 when his daughter was born, and his wife Leah is listed as a widow in the 1910 US census. It is possible that the whole group was alive and in Odessa in 1897 when my Grandfather Alexander Barad was born there, so with luck, the census records may yield all their names and even the street address(es) where they lived.

So, I am very excited to be joining Galina's list (kindly confirm my registration and number) and hopeful Galina can assist with at least a few exciting breakthroughs for my family history research.

Regards,
--Bob

Note from Bob (March 31, 2014)

"Galina came through. Months later, she sent me a photocopy of David Nathan Barad's sister Polina Barad's birth record. Polina was duly recorded in the registry as the daughter of Nathan and Leah Barad, together with one more newfound gem: the birth record revealed that, as suspected, the earliest Barads were not from Odessa but had originated further inland, from the town of Novogard-Volynsk.

"That is where the recorded line of Barad family history starts, at least until another mind forever voyaging picks up the search and advances it further. When they do, I suspect the next clues may not lie on paper but inside our own bodies, recorded in the human serial numbering system known as the Y chromosome DNA. It will probably be through these living memories that, eventually, everything is illuminated.

"As mom says, 'life is for the living.' She's right. But living is just part of the deal. The memory of things past is also our task, together with our responsibility to pass these stories forward to future generations. So, thank you, Wayne, for taking such an essential part in preserving Dick's too-short life, and with it, so many precious memories. Through remembering, we demonstrate our hope for a future that shines even brighter under the lights of the past, and with the conviction that time's best jewels are most honored by how we choose to live in the present."

Appendix W

Leah Barad the First
from Bob Barad (March 30, 2014)

After my son Richard's Bar Mitzvah and the search for our missing Uncle Uszer, I continued exploring family history. I read the detailed written accounts from cousin Adele and Uncle Emil, and I wondered if the Internet could again turn up something extra. Using Dot's Ancestry.com account, I identified U. S. census records confirming locations and members of Krival and Barad households through the first decades of the 20th century. Checking microfilm lent to me in Rome by the local branch of the Mormon Church, I read the transcript of David Nathan Barad's naturalization hearing held in Kings County (Brooklyn) New York that led to his becoming a U. S. citizen in the 1890s. And I continued browsing the Ellis Island passenger manifests, trying alternate spellings of 'Barad.'

It was through one of those Ellis Island searches that I located the passenger manifest recording great-great grandmother Leah Barad's arrival in the U. S. in 1905. Her name was not retained in family memories, so it was an exciting discovery (not least to Leah Barad the Second who, up until that time, everyone assumed was Leah Barad the First). But this first Leah's link to son David Nathan Barad was conclusive – his name and the 1910 U. S. census-verified Brooklyn address are written on the scanned Ellis Island passenger manifest as her travel destination.

Reading between the lines, there were probably good reasons that memories of this family reunion were not recorded for future generations: Leah was in the last years of her life and was fleeing from an Odessa that was no longer safe for Jews, who had once thrived there. Just one month after Leah Barad landed in the New World, the Old World she had known disintegrated in the October 1905 Pogrom, the worst and most decisive effort to extinguish Jewish life in that commercial port city.

I had always heard that my dad's family was from Odessa, but reading about its history, I discovered that "being from Odessa" was a lot like saying your family "comes from Las Vegas." In the 1820s, when David Nathan Barad's paternal grandparents were likely born, the former Turkish fortress town turned into a Russian city by order of Catherine the Great was less than 30 years old.

Going back to the Internet for answers, I discovered a group mailing list of Jews with Odessa roots that had joined forces online to search for their early family histories. The list was run by Anita Citron who had secured a source inside the Odessa State Archives, a Ukrainian woman named Galina who, for a reasonable fee, would search the surviving synagogue birth registries recorded by the Jewish community of 19th century Odessa and share its secrets. But there was a waiting list for obtaining Galina's assistance. So, hopefully, I explained my research objectives, paid the required advance fee and took a number…

(Thank you to Dot, our modern-day Barad archivist, for saving these emails.)

Acknowledgements:

This would have been impossible to compile without the help of every one mentioned above. I won't try to list them all here because I have clearly identified them in the text.

But there are several people I must thank.

First, my wife, Lorrie. She understood the passion this aroused in me from the very beginning. She supported me at every turn, pause, discovery, and plateau. And she willingly did the layout because technologically-challenged me didn't know how. Without her support and cooperation, this would not have come to fruition.

My daughters, Katie and Kelsey, who were both living at home when I began this odyssey and who are both now "out in the world." Thanks for understanding why I had to do this.

To my friend, author John Calu for his insight and support. And to author Corinne H. Smith, who took the time to read this manuscript at various stages of construction and who offered such invaluable advice that this book would not be in the shape that it is without her. I didn't mean for you to become my personal editor, but I'm eternally grateful that you did. This mere "thank you" can never repay you for how much support you gave, but thank you.

To Bob Barad, whose painstaking attention to detail is truly appreciated. His contributions make this a much more precise story. You came late to this dance but your contributions are heartfelt, and I thank you for them.

Jackie Herbert Marks for allowing me to take her back to one of the most private times of her life, and not hating me for asking her, repeatedly, to write about it.

Nancy Scattergood Donavan, for revisiting what has to be the most juxtaposed time of her life: the joy of life with Dick and the birth of Leah, and the death of her husband literally in front of her eyes, a widowed mother of a not-yet-one-year-old girl. As you described it to me, a "numbing year." Thank you for walking me through the joy and the pain. You're a superstar in this story.

Dr. Jerry and Mrs. Bea Barad who did not want to go down this path originally, but I thank them for their trust, and support, and opening their hearts and memories to me. I printed a hard copy of the first draft of this book and put it in spiral notebooks for them to read which they did before each one passed away. They liked it. You are both sorely missed.

All of Dick's grade school, high school, and college buddies who contributed.

David and Dot Barad. How brave to trust someone so much out on the periphery to take on the most private and personal remembrances. Your contributions were immeasurable, as was the evident love for your brother and the protective nature with which you both journeyed through this project. My admiration for both of you knows no bounds. If the roles were reversed, I am not sure that I would have placed so much trust in you as you did in me, and I am grateful for that trust.

And, finally, Leah. You are your father's (and mother's) daughter. Those of us who knew your dad see him when we see you. Remember when you got to Cornell and you wrote, "I wonder if anyone here resembles my dad?" and your mom wrote: "Leah, look in the mirror!" You have spent your life wondering about your dad and trying to find out what kind of person he was, and how much of him you carry in yourself. I hope this has helped you to see for yourself what the rest of us already know: you are Dick's daughter. I am not slighting your mother in any way when I say that, and I'm sure she knows that.

The overriding principle I maintained in this effort was to paint a picture in words of what Dick was like for you. I hope I helped you to understand your family history as well as the kind of person your dad was.

During your lifetime, I am sure you will meet someone who is committed, dedicated, opinionated, fun-loving, yet disciplined. When you do, you just met the kind of man your dad was.

We all loved him.

Be wise, know yourself, and have a good life.

Wayne T. Dilts
January 15, 2017

Notes and Sources
Notes:

David believes that the picture of Dot, Dick and himself atop a horse that can be found on Jerry's Facebook page was taken at the Zeng farm.

Sources:

Much of this information came from emails from David, Dot and Bob Barad, but I also acknowledge the time and patience given to me and my seemingly endless questions by everyone else.

All photos included in this book came from members of the immediate Barad family. Due to the age of many of them, photo credits were not available.

The information about Mr. Zeng's death in an airline crash can be seen at http://en.wikipedia.org/wiki/Eastern_Air_Lines_Flight_304

The site that contains information about the legend of a John Ringo buried treasure is
http://books.google.com/books?id=ww7BJbdR4lEC&pg=PA309&lpg=PA309&dq=treasure+hunt+ringoes&source=bl&ots=Ewm_igdA8x&sig=f-uD95Y6YfstpT9dAzpctOBWJAU&hl=en&ei=mzk_TZmRIJD2swOzxuGzBQ&sa=X&oi=book_result&ct=result&resnum=1&sqi=2&ved=0CBMQ6AEwAA#v=onepage&q=treasure%20hunt%20ringoes&f=false

The Echo. HCHS yearbook, 1970.

Hunterdon County Democrat, The (HCD). "Mrs. Rose Angell First To Decide County Should and Could Have Its Own Hospital." 25 June 1953. Sec 1, page 1; section 5, page 1.

Katcher, Avrum L., M.D. *A Time to Remember*. Hunterdon Medical Center Foundation, 2003.

Matteson, John. *The Lives of Margaret Fuller*. New York: Norton, 2012.

In-person interviews:

Barad, David. New York City, NY. April 12, 2012.
Barad, Jerry and Bea (with David and Dot). Flemington, NJ. June 5, 2011.
Barad, Dorothy. Telephone interview. January 26, 2014.
Donavan, Nancy Scattergood (with Peter Donavan, Leah Barad, and Dot Barad). Bennington, VT. October 8, 2011.
Moncrief, Robert. Flemington, NJ, August 7, 2011.

ABOUT THE AUTHOR

Wayne T. Dilts is now retired from a 28-year career as a high school English teacher in New Jersey. He has been married to his wife Lorraine Gilrane Dilts for 33 years and they have two grown daughters: Katie, currently a law student at McGeorge School of Law in Sacramento, California; and Kelsey, who currently works for FEMA and is a member of the US Army Reserves.

Mr. Dilts previously edited two books by his father-in-law, Thomas Gilrane: *Just The Way It Was* (2007) and *Rambling With Tom* (2016).

Mr. Dilts can be contacted by email at wdilts@hotmail.com

42798780R00120

Made in the USA
Middletown, DE
21 April 2017